Praise for *The State of Play*

"If you want to explain to anyone why video games are worth caring about, this is a single-volume primer on where we are, how we got here, and where we're going next. In every way, this is the state of play."
—KIERON GILLEN, author of *The Wicked + The Divine*,
    co-founder of Rock, Paper, Shotgun

"Video games are now on the front lines of the culture wars. *The State of Play* gathers essential voices who are trying to make a more just, more true, more playful gamespace, one that's fun for everybody."
—MCKENZIE WARK, author of *Gamer Theory*

"*The State of Play* is an excellent primer [and] a much-needed alternative look at the state and stakes of video game culture, today and tomorrow."
—ANGELA WASHKO, artist and founder of The Council on Gender
    Sensitivity and Behavioral Awareness in *World of Warcraft*

"We are past the era when it was surprising to learn that video games are more than just pleasurable power fantasies. Video games are emotional explorations of race, gender, sex and love. Video games give us intense experiences of being others, or finding ourselves, alone with the computer or surrounded by crowds, in physical or virtual spaces. *The State of Play* is a key collection of writings to understand why playing video games matters more than ever."
—MIGUEL ANGEL SICART, author of *Play Matters* and *The Ethics of
    Computer Games*

"Like a game that opens your heart, I found more than I came for in *The State of Play*. . . . Not what I expected, but much more. The thoughtful, articulate essays recursively confirm the importance of gaming to society, the book's key theme. Beautifully written in workmanlike, accessible prose, and highly recommended."
—BONNIE NARDI, author of *My Life as a Night Elf Priest: An Anthropological Account of* World of Warcraft

"This highly recommended edition is not just about the state of play, it is about so much more: the state of everything digital—by way of video games, in spite of them, transcending them. Yes, indeed: games are f****** political."
—DR. STEFFEN P. WALZ, co-editor of *The Gameful World*

"This diverse collection demonstrates the deep power of anchoring our design theories in the lived experiences of players and creators. It offers a kaleidoscopic view of the possibility space of games, providing exciting new perspectives on play and the construction of play spaces."
—BRIAN UPTON, author of *The Aesthetic of Play*

"Through a combination of deeply personal narratives and academic analyses *The State of Play* effectively illuminates the social and cultural relevance of gaming. . . . The authors do not simply discuss what games are technically, but what they are, can, and should be culturally."
—ELLEN MIDDAUGH, co-editor of *#youthaction: Becoming Political in the Digital Age*

THE STATE OF PLAY

CREATORS AND CRITICS ON VIDEO GAME CULTURE

IAN BOGOST • LEIGH ALEXANDER • ZOE QUINN
ANITA SARKEESIAN & KATHERINE CROSS • IAN SHANAHAN
ANNA ANTHROPY • EVAN NARCISSE • HUSSEIN IBRAHIM
CARA ELLISON & BRENDAN KEOGH • DAN GOLDING
DAVID JOHNSTON • WILLIAM KNOBLAUCH
MERRITT KOPAS • OLA WIKANDER

EDITED BY

DANIEL GOLDBERG & LINUS LARSSON

Seven Stories Press
NEW YORK • OAKLAND

A Seven Stories Press First Edition

Seven Stories Press
140 Watts Street
New York, NY 10013
www.sevenstories.com

College professors may order examination copies of Seven Stories Press titles for free. To order, visit http://www.sevenstories.com/textbook or send a fax on school letterhead to (212) 226-1411.

Book design by Elizabeth DeLong and Jon Gilbert

Library of Congress Cataloging-in-Publication Data
The state of play : sixteen voices on video games / edited by Daniel Goldberg and Linus Larsson. -- First edition.
     pages cm
  ISBN 978-1-60980-639-2 (hardcover)
  1. Video games--Social aspects. I. Goldberg, Dan (Daniel) II. Larsson, Linus.
  GV1469.34.S52S73 2015
  794.8--dc23
                    2015004641

Printed in the United States

9 8 7 6 5 4 3 2 1

Contents

Introduction

Post-Escapism:
A New Discourse on
Video Game Culture

DANIEL GOLDBERG & LINUS LARSSON

ASK ANYONE YOU MEET ON THE STREET AND CHANCES ARE they will have spent more time in the past week or month playing video games than reading books or magazines. A few short decades ago, video games were considered a niche hobby for nerds and computer geeks. Today, they are an inseparable part of global popular culture. Video games are everywhere, played by people of all ages, faiths, and nationalities. Game design is taught in schools next to architecture, photography, and fashion. Big budget video games often surpass Hollywood blockbusters in terms of both production budgets and profitability.

And yet, video game culture has been reluctant to step out of the boys' room. There are of course historical exceptions (for example, see William Knoblauch on the subtle anti-war subtexts of many Cold War-era video games, page 183), but unlike, say, music or literature, games have no strong tradition of engaging with social issues, politics, or the culture that surrounds them. Game designers have historically eschewed reality and the present day for the fantastical and imaginary, with light-hearted science fiction, fantasy, and fairy-tale settings as staples of the form. Many argue that escapism is precisely the point.

There are historical reasons for this. More than any other form of creative expression, video games are highly dependent on, and to a certain extent an offshoot of, advances in computing and digital technology. This means games have traditionally been engaged with and discussed as products of technology rather than products of culture, which is why most game criticism still tends to read a lot like a review of a mobile phone or a car. The specialist gaming press has a long tradition of consumer-oriented criticism, using simple, quantifiable parameters to measure the technical proficiency and craftsmanship of the game designer, the "fun level" of a game, and the "value for the money" that a game provides. How smooth are the animations? How sophisticated are the graphics? How well-balanced are the rules?

Video game production has historically been prohibitively expensive and time-consuming, giving big-name publishers a virtual monopoly on production, sales, and marketing. As a result, the cultural identity of the "gamer" was from an early stage largely appropriated and shaped by the dominant corporate interests of the industry. This created a consumption-centric culture with its own norms and value systems, clustered around a small number of brands and big-budget franchises while showing little concern for identities other than the prime demographic of the young, white, Western male.

But in recent years the barriers of entry into the industry have lowered considerably. Digital distribution platforms such as Steam and the Apple App Store have made it infinitely easier for small-scale video game productions to reach a large audience. Cheap and widely available game-making tools (see, for example, anna anthropy, page 33, for more on Twine) have made it possible for those without a degree in computer science to approach game design as a form of creative expression. This has helped give rise to a thriving scene of independent game development next to the Tolkien-esque fantasy epics and chart-topping military-themed shooters of the dominant publishers. The indie scene of today is perhaps best described as an experimental greenhouse feeding off the audience of the established industry while providing fresh talent and new ideas.

Recently, a new generation of independent video game designers have begun to explore how games can be used for social and political activism and commentary. Topics such as sexism, race, politics, and class injustice are today being grappled with to an extent that has previously been absent from the form. For example, anna anthropy (see page 33) recounts her experiences of hormone replacement therapy in *Dys4ia*. In *Cart Life*, Richard Hofmeier examines the relentless churning of Western capitalism through the lives and actions of American street vendors. In *Depression Quest*, Zoe Quinn (see page 85) attempts to immerse the player in her own experiences of clinical depression.

These three examples are all in some way autobiographical. They aspire to make a point about how their creators perceive the world around them, and interactivity gives them the power to do so in ways that are impossible for creators in other fields. *Cart Life* doesn't just describe life in poverty; it forces players to engage with and immerse themselves in it. If you only had money for one, would you feed your cat or yourself? If you had to choose, would you work late so you could afford to pay rent, or would you leave on time so you could pick your daughter up after school?

What's more, these games do not easily slot into preexisting categories or genres. For example, while there exists no official definition of the term *serious games*, it is often applied to games whose primary purpose is something other than entertainment. It may refer to games that are created for education, marketing, professional training, or to advance a certain political standpoint. This, by definition, means they are exercises in communications or public relations above all, simply borrowing game design mechanics as a way to make their point. In contrast, the examples above are games first and foremost, created independently. They represent an evolution of the form rather than a reappropriation of its mechanics.

Games such as these have helped foster a new school of video game criticism with particular interest in gender and identity politics. The work of Anita Sarkeesian (see page 103) has spearheaded a growing movement of feminist critical analysis of games. Other writers have begun examining the (mis)representation of non-straight, non-white, and non-Western minorities in gaming (see Evan Narcisse, page 53; and Hussein Ibrahim, page 77), or the common emphasis on violence as a core game mechanic (see Cara Ellison and Brendan Keogh, page 141).

These developments point toward a philosophical shift in the perception of what games are and ought to be. There is, it seems, a newfound willingness among both game designers and critics to engage with games in the context of the world they exist in, as opposed to considering them in a vacuum devoid of social or political forces. In other words, video game culture is finally starting to grow up.

In early 2004, game writer Kieron Gillen coined the influential phrase "New Games Journalism." Taking his cue from writers such as Tom Wolfe and Hunter S. Thompson, he envisioned a new kind of criticism that emphasized the subjective experiences of the player, essentially arguing that the worth of a video game lies not in the game but in the gamer (for a defining example of the form, see Ian Shanahan, page 25). Today, perhaps a similarly useful definition is that the discourse on games is moving into a state of post-escapism—that is, a discourse that looks for meaning beyond entertainment and the joy of play. New Games Journalism sought to understand games through the subjective experiences of the player. Post-escapism understands games by placing them in social, political, and cultural context. It finds value in what a game says about the world around it.

Like all progressive movements, these developments have been met with a backlash. At its ugliest, this has manifested in the hate mob behavior of Gamergate, named after the Twitter hashtag #gamergate that first emerged during summer 2014 and that has since snowballed into a loosely defined online movement (for more on this topic, see Dan Golding, page 127).

On a basic level, Gamergate has functioned as a focal point for the rampant misogyny that has plagued tech and online culture for decades. Several prominent game designers and critics, almost exclusively women, have been targeted with slander and threats of violence, sexual assault, and outright murder for speaking their minds on these topics (see Anita Sarkeesian and Katherine Cross, page 103; and Zoe Quinn, page 85). This, of course, deserves only to be condemned. But Gamergate can also be understood as a reactionary counterforce to the ongoing and rapid maturation of video game culture, and to the progressive voices that are embracing these changes.

Controversies around video games are nothing new. The form has been under intense scrutiny for decades and vilified for everything from glorifying violence to promoting drug-like addiction among the young. But these accusations have most often come from the outside—from politicians, pundits, and academics with little or no inside understanding of the culture. Gamergate is notable because it is, perhaps for the first time, an attack by one group within video game culture on another. At its core, it represents a civil war for control over the future discourse on games. On one side are designers and critics arguing that games should be viewed as meaningful tools for understanding the world around us and the interplay between human beings, borrowing heavily from progressive and emancipatory movements such as feminism. On the other side are conservative voices wishing for a return to an imagined, perhaps mid-'90s utopia largely exempt from critical analysis beyond the purely technical, thus leaving old norms and hierarchies to stand largely unchallenged.

In reality, video games are a complex and rapidly evolving form, where different qualities intertwine and influence each other in subtle, often surprising ways. A progressive, critical approach to games and their place in culture does not preclude the appreciation of them as the rich and wonderful pieces of entertainment they are. But if our understanding of them is to move beyond simple escapism, games must be held up to the same standards and allowed the same scrutiny as any other form of creative expression.

Our hope is that this anthology may play a small part in furthering that understanding. It contains essays by sixteen of the most powerful and unique progressive voices in gaming today, on subjects ranging from gender, race, and identity to sex, violence, and faith. Taken as a whole these essays emphasize how the conversation around games is changing from holding an unrelenting focus on technology and mechanics to not being afraid to engage with worlds outside its own. If art is defined as a lens through which we perceive reality, then games are just beginning their transition from artifacts of technology into something more.

ADVENT

LEIGH ALEXANDER

For three decades or more, video games have been the most widespread form of children's entertainment in the developed world. Even so, they remain absent from most depictions of childhood in contemporary literature. In *Breathing Machine: A Memoir of Computers*—from which this essay is an excerpt—Leigh Alexander provides an exception and breaks fresh ground by giving an intimate and highly personal account of the relationship between the child, game, and machine.

A LUMINESCENT GREEN PROMPT BLINKS SOFTLY AT ME like an eye. I'm in the basement, and there is the humming of machines. In an alcove, the clothes dryer repeats a soft, rhythmic thudding. I curl up so my toes don't touch the chilly floor.

There's no disk in the drive. I left it empty on purpose, an open mouth crowned with an angry red eye. Its inside parts stutter and whirr within their beige casing. A sound barks from it like a scolding, but I already know it won't hurt me.

Everything is green lines, green light. An altar, a yawning vacuum of black, glassy space, a box with a screen, and on the screen there's a tiny, vivid green rectangle flashing slowly in place. I press my little face up closer to the monitor, and I can see the flashing rectangle is built of tiny, impeccable lines etched one atop the other, the lines themselves comprised of infinitesimal dots.

The precise language of computers and programming might as well have been magic spells. Trying to brute-force my way into arcane conversation with machines was like feeling my way along a dark closet wall, hoping to stumble into Narnia. I did plenty of that fumbling for Narnia: this button, this ritual, this combination of objects would—oh, it had to, it must—let me escape this little world, where everyone yelled at me about math.

I promised my cousin we could teleport to a museum at night if we said the right words. I promised my sister we'd fight crime just as soon as I could build a portable AI. I promised my classmates on the playground that there were invisible tribes in the woods. We would summon mermaids if we arranged a set of stones just so.

I feared the word "no," its very self. I hated to be thwarted. By the time I was in fourth grade, the teacher had already called my parents more than once to say they did not think I could tell fantasy from reality.

I could tell. I could. I just didn't want to. I don't want to, I don't want to, I wailed, I marched out to the hallway bench. Again.

My earliest memories are of the breathing machines, and how they promised from the time I was born that anything could exist, that all things were solvable, that anything could be brought into striking, vector-lined reality if you had imagination enough. There was always someplace else to go than here, where I had to do math and wear a neon scrunchie for dance class.

My father wrote a "home technology" column for the Boston Globe in the early 1980s, when technology in the home was a novelty in and of itself. He wrote about hi-fis and that somehow led to an uncurated heap of press materials barraging our house continually. We were sent hardware and software in plastic-wrapped boxes the size, thickness, and weight of novels. They had dramatic sci-fi cover paintings—vast, elaborate box art on the outside, and clumsily-blipped eight-bit shorthand adventures inside.

Dad thought I should learn computers as a child to be employable as an adult. My access to them was virtually uninhibited, except for when I was yelled at for accidentally erasing this or that. Otherwise I was constantly enshrined in front of the Apple][e, mashing keys, engaged in lawless, experimental dialogue with a machine.

From the mysterious boxes piled in our office closet, I pulled and prized black floppy disks with bright labels and sticky, flimsy black-tape bellies I knew never to touch. Each disk was shorthand for an adventure—they had names like *Critical Mass*, *Mystery House*, *Ring Quest*, *Blade of Blackpoole*, *Kabul Spy*, and *Death in the Caribbean*.

Those old things were blunt objects, the kind that make you think about how many tiny edges must have existed all over the surface of the very first wheel. Slowly, there emerged a line drawing loads, etching a graphic abstraction of a path, house, or forest into the black mirror of your boxy computer screen. You are an international spy. You must find the wizard. You are standing outside the house. You are on a path facing EAST. Things like that would be all you were given to know about yourself and the world.

You would type N for North, and often YOU CAN'T GO THAT WAY would be the stern rebuke. GO NORTH, you'd patiently enter, and if you were lucky, you'd get back a line or two about how the mountains barred your way, or how the impassable woods sprawled forever in that direction. CLIMB TREES, I would insist. Or I'd try, CLIMB THE MOUNTAINS.

YOU CAN'T DO THAT, the world inside the machine would insist in return, or I DON'T UNDERSTAND.

Some games understood climbing, some did not. Some let you press I to view your inventory (a lamp, a letter, or nothing whatsoever), and some required you to type the entire word, INVENTORY. I learned so many words from games: GULLY, SLUICE, BRAZIER, ADUMBRATE, OGRESS, EGRESS (which I thought was another kind of ogre).

For a child who hated to hear "no" so badly, I never heard it so eloquently than from the leaden mouths of those ancient worlds. Their blunt denials kept me up at night—the locked gate whose key I couldn't locate, the vile and crudely-animated manticore whose appetite I couldn't figure out how to slake, the endless and constant grisly deaths I couldn't manage to avoid.

So often, it was a matter of the right answer and the precise right phrasing. These games were finicky about their syntax— TIE ROPE, you'd demand, and TO WHAT, it would ask, then TO TREE would confuse it, but merely answering TREE would not. It was always, always possible that you had the right answer to the puzzle, but the wrong words, the wrong verbs.

At seven years old, I would sit bolt upright on the verge of sleep, struck suddenly by a solution in the dark of my room, waiting for morning and my next attempt with uncontainable excitement in a kind of fever.

I'd imagine what new lands waited beyond the sequences I couldn't complete, so fervently that even now I can't remember if they were real. My neighbor Charlotte (of the scientist father and the basement full of spellbooks) and I would constantly plot, collaborate, and imagine, spending those hot summer afternoons when school was out sitting side by side at a machine.

At her house lived a monolithic, primitive PC the size of a refrigerator. It was 1988 and there was one particular pizza-sized disk we'd tuck into its shelf-sized jaw at every opportunity. At the command prompt, Charlotte would type ADVENT to run the game. She hit those letters like a religious hymn.

This particular game was called *Colossal Cave Adventure*, a text-only network of caves and treasures that sprawled like a tomb of hieroglyphs so truly massive and confounding that I've not solved it to this day, which feels right.

Digital historians call *Colossal Cave Adventure* the "granddaddy" of text adventure games. A spelunker named Will Crowther made it for his daughters to help share his cave-crawling pastime with them while he endured a divorce with his wife. His work parented me and Charlotte through those summers, in a different era. It felt like we could lock ourselves away and go absent for hours without making our parents nervous.

Much of our playtime was spent concentrating on the game itself, rubber-cementing reams of printer paper end to end to map the cave and its strange place names: Bedquilt, the Hall of the Mountain King, mazes of identical twisting passages, an alcove where a hollow voice cried "Plugh." The virtual cave network contained a Ming vase, a set of batteries, a bent rod crowned with a rusty star and all kinds of objects to be collected for some inexplicable purpose.

The rest of the time, we tumbled forth into our real-life suburban wildlands, the scraggly woods between one grassy yard and another, and the tiny duck pond that still looms large in my memory. Everywhere, it seemed, we saw a puzzle, a mystery. Why was that bundle of twigs leaning against an old oak? Why did some stones glitter when you struck them, and others stank of gunpowder? Under this log, a salamander, and under that, a nest of beetles. There were loamy, unseen living things always scuttling just out of reach. We left notes and signs wherever we could get away with it, and it felt like important work.

This knothole could be a button. Behold this twig stripped of its bark and written on by termites—a magic staff! The things that lay beyond our reach in the digital world seemed to mirror and echo the natural mysteries we found when we played outdoors. At the end of the day, I'd be in trouble for the mud on my shoes or for coming home a little too late, but I always tromped into the front door feeling like I was almost, almost somewhere. Like I'd almost solved it, whatever "it" really was.

There were, there had to be, gorgeous infrastructures beyond what I could reach, just waiting for me to know the right words. The whole world was a blinking prompt, daring me, ENTER COMMAND.

Leigh Alexander's writing on the business and culture of video games has appeared in Wired, The New Statesman, The Guardian, Polygon, *and numerous other publications.*

Bow, Nigger

IAN SHANAHAN

What you are about to read is, in a way, what started and defined it all. Originally published under Ian Shanahan's online pseudonym, Always Black, "Bow, Nigger" is a key text in the canon of what is now known as New Games Journalism. It was one of the earliest pieces to grapple with how digital identity is expressed in multiplayer games, and it is widely considered one of the most influential critiques of video game culture, ever.

"BOW, NIGGER," HE TYPED.

I kind of hunched uncomfortably over the keyboard at that point. Not that I should've taken offence, really.

For one thing, my screen name has nothing to do with my ethnicity. For another, it's only a game and the fascist doing the typing is probably hundreds of miles away and far beyond anything you could call an actual influence on my life.

But still . . . It's not very nice, is it?

What to do?

I circled around him warily.

Jedi Knight II: Jedi Outcast does one thing very, very well, and that's lightsabres. In fact, it's probably more accurate to say George Lucas et al did lightsabres very well in the *Star Wars* films and *Outcast* does a good job of recalling the memory of those flashing contests. The emulation is near perfect, from the initial hiss as light slowly rises from the handle, to the sweeping motion-blurred visuals and the threatening, pitch-shifting hum.

Throughout the game, you can choose which perspective to view the action from. The game defaults to first-person for projectile weapons but drawing your lightsabre switches to third-person ass-cam and this is by far the best configuration. Leave it alone.

Third-person allows you to fully appreciate the acrobatics of the sabre fighting animations. You can swing away in one of three styles: fast, medium, and heavy, all of which allow you wrestle mouse movement and direction key presses to produce jaw-dropping combinations of slashes, chops, and stabs that risk you forgetting any question of your actual opponent as you stare in disbelief and whisper, "Did I just do that?"

"Bow," he types.

Hmm. Problem. For all of the excellent swordplay animations, Raven seems to have omitted any of the more mundane actions you could imagine your avatar performing. There is no "Bow" button.

What my socially belligerent friend is being so insistent about is something else, and that's a form of "physical" expression that grew out of the enthusiasm of some of the more ardent Star Wars fans who play *JKII* online. Some people take their fiction VERY seriously and wannabe Jedi Knights are among the most serious. The faithful, in order to be more true to the Jedi Code of Honour, crouch before each other and duck their "heads" down as a mark of respect before entering into battle. Some people think that's silly.

I thought it was silly, the first time I saw it. Then I saw everybody was doing it. And then I felt silly not doing it. It's strange how much weight the actions of your peers can bring to bear on you, even when your social medium is only a bunch of really fast math on a German server.

I'm currently in heavy style. This affords me the most damaging attacks at the expense of much slower swings. When you're not attacking, it also provides the best defense, parrying is handled automatically. The best defense is wise while I'm facing off with this wanker. We've been engaged in our duel for two or three minutes and neither one of us has come close enough to hit each other yet. This is a period of sizing up.

Sometimes rash headlong attacks can be exploited by a player of a reasonable skill level, and you'll find yourself ghosting and waiting for another turn before you know what hit you. If you've never played a particular opponent before, it pays to feel him out a bit.

First, though, there are the formalities. I crouch and duck my head in a "bow." Vulnerable.

Stupid? Yeah.

But you know what? I entered in to it willingly and "why?" is a very interesting question.

I'm a big boy now and I don't want to be a Jedi Knight when I grow up. The Star Wars films are great, but they're also just that, films—a form of entertainment to be enjoyed during breaks from my very real and financially challenging life (mortgage, two cats, a broken gutter and a car that needs some attention. Cheers.)

So I didn't bow because I wanted to role-play as a Jedi. It was an act of defiance.

Duelling is not new. Any multiplayer game can leave you with one opponent on either side, and I've played that scenario out in many games. The difference with lightsabre duelling, *Outcast*-style, is that it's so very personal. These aren't detached sniping matches across the width of the map, or rocket-spamming blast-fests to see who can respawn the least. *JKII* duel is winner-stays-on, and you can be floating around for anything up to half an hour on a busy server waiting for a game. This makes your game life actually worth something, and it makes it worth fighting for.

Into this potent mix, you can toss in the fact that while you're a ghosting spectator you have time to chat and actually get to know the people you're playing, even on that usually most impersonal of beasts, the public server. During actual fights, play can swing from bouts of thrust, slash and parry to more distant and wary sizing-up in search of an opening that will allow you to land a sucker-hit before your opponent can counter. There's time to talk and taunt.

But perhaps most personal of all is the close proximity you have to come to damage your opponent. I'm an avoidant player at the best of times, but *JKII* lightsabre duels don't allow you to hit and fade from range. You have to be right in there trying to give the other guy a laser enema if you're going to avoid watching the show for another six games.

So I bowed. Not because I was naive enough to think he'd give any significance to the gesture. Not because he was commanding me to from his pillar of arrogance. I bowed despite his taunts. For all his goading, I did "the right thing" to show him I wasn't going to come and meet him down on his level.

Blammo.

SONOFABITCH! Jesus, all my shields and forty health are lost from one big heavy-stance overhead chop before he spins away, back to the other side of the map.

"LOL! Nigger."

He goes into a "blender." Every style has a selection of special moves that can activated by combination key presses; these are set pieces taken from notable moments of the films. Unfortunately, because *JKII* is based on the *Quake III* engine, the macro scripting of that seminal of all first-person shooters is easily migrated across. This means that all skill or effort can be eliminated from the execution of these moves by a few simple scripts that can be readily downloaded and bound to a key. A blender is the heavy-stance backsweep move, or several rather, chained together, causing the model to spin unrealistically like a top. It's fatal if you get too near it, but very difficult to use in an actual fight, since you're unable to do anything until the animation has finished. It's a shame that exploits like this would eventually lead to the ultimate downfall of the multiplayer game.

He's showboating. He's demonstrating how 1337 he is.

"Are you really black nigger?" he types.

"Why?" I replied.

"Because it matters," he says.

I ignore that and edge closer by a circuitous route. I don't want to get caught out by one of his lame keybinds. I switch down to medium stance, my favorite and the best balance between speed and damage.

"I know I hurt you by the things I say," he says.

I hit T to talk and the chat icon appears above my head. But I hesitate. I want to say something, but with the little underscore blinking away, my fingers stop over the keys. Say what? "No, you don't"; "No, you aren't"; "How can you when your insults are meaningless?"; "Fuck you, asshole"?

And SLASH. Bastard.

In chat mode you're powerless, like most other games. Your typing fingers can't do much about an assault by a conscienceless typekiller. In all my years of twitch-gaming, my fingers have never moved so fast across the keyboard, escaping the trap of chat mode to rally my defenses against his lightning fast slashes.

Almost too late, I put distance between us. Almost too late, but not quite. Five health points remain and I know I haven't even hit him yet. Five health means you're nearly dead. A brush from the tip of a sabre held idly will remove five health points from you and take you out of the game. Shit.

It's really, really unfair. I mean, alright, I've asked for it, haven't I? I was aware from the outset what kind of player I was facing, and still I insisted on performing the ritual courtesies, and still I fell for the oldest trick in the book, cut to ribbons while I answered a pointless taunt. I've only myself to blame.

For the most part *JKII* multiplayer isn't like that. Mostly, *JKII* players are like players everywhere, they just want to have a blast and enjoy the competition. They'll show each other a degree of respect that is absent from most other multiplayer games, and they express that respect in a variety of ways, from the odd little emergent bow to ad hoc lessons from complete strangers, to clans adopting the padawan-master relationship outlined in the films. Most of the players are good guys.

This is why it was unfair. The game allows "bad behavior," and this is a good thing. It means that by avoiding "bad" behavior you can demonstrate how "good" you are. Virtuous. A lack of virtue is unfairness in the unofficial rules of the game but the only answer you have is to fight back. You too can be unfair, but, um, some people don't like to play that way. They make a choice.

This one makes his choice. This one is a bad guy, and he isn't messing about anymore. I guess he's run out of tricks, or perhaps he's done a few quick mental calculations and realized that I'm probably on the ropes, because he starts spamming the heavy-stance finishing move informally termed "Death From Above."

This begins with a long flat leap and ends with an overhead chop. Get caught under it and it's fatal no matter how many shield or health points you have left.

Which is a mistake on his part. It's total overkill, even though he doesn't know I only have five health points left. I happen to know that the very end of "Death From Above" leaves you very vulnerable indeed. He has underestimated me and who can blame him? I've hardly been the epitome of laser swordsmanship thus far. I'll fix that impression just now.

A quick swap down to fast style and a crouch-forward attack puts me into a lunge, catching him with an uppercut. It's by no means fatal, but I rock his world there for a moment. He thought he was dominating, and now he's lost a whole lot of health and he wasn't ready for that.

He actually reels. There's always scope for projecting a little extra personification onto a computer-generated character, but I swear to god he has shock on his face. Entirely too rash for my current health level, I go into a little whirlwind of fast-style slashes and probably ding him a little more in the process as he beats a hasty retreat.

No chatting now. No more insults. Collision detection in *JKII* is a little flaky. Sometimes hits do far more damage than you might have thought. I can hope. He comes at me and we have at it.

The lightsabres hiss and fizz when they come into contact with each other. I roll and dodge and parry for all I'm worth. Five health only, nearly dead.

A little something personal about myself: I don't sweat. Never have. Not under normal, sit-at-the-computer circumstances anyway. Obviously, physical exertion makes me sweat—running, jumping, swimming, etc. But not just sitting in a chair.

We spin around each other, bouncing off the furniture of the map. My concentration is absolutely intense and never before have I tried so hard to "be the mouse." I feel a trickle of sweat run down from under my right armpit.

You see what this has become? It's not just a trivial game to be played in an idle moment, but a genuine battle of good versus evil. It has nothing to do with Star Wars or Jedi Knights, or any of the fluff that surrounds the game's mechanics. I played by the rules and he didn't—that makes me the "good" guy and him the "baddie," but this is real, in the sense that there's no telling who's going to win out here. There's no script or plot to determine the eventual triumph of the good guy (that's me, five health); there's no natural order of a fictional universe, or any question of an apocryphal ultimate balance. There's just me and him, light and dark, in a genuine contest between the two.

And there it is. I don't even know what. Some chance slash or poke in all of the rolling and jumping around and his lifeless avatar, with all his racist stabs and underhand duplicity, goes tumbling to the floor, vanquished by the guy who, even in the face of all of that, played by the rules. Only one health point remains but I win.

I'm a fucking hero. A real one.

A beep and a server message: Wanker has disconnected.

I can only dream of the howls of anguish so far away.

My next opponent spawns. And bows. A chat icon appears. "Awesome," he types.

Ian Shanahan is a video game journalist based in the United Kingdom.

Love, Twine, and the End of the World

ANNA ANTHROPY

Few video game designers can be said to truly make games that attempt to redefine the form. anna anthropy is one of them. Her work regularly questions the purpose of video games and challenges conventional choices of subject matter. Here, through the story of how her game *Queers In Love at the End of the World* came to be, she explores possibilites for non-programmers to make games themselves using Twine, an online tool for creating text-based adventures.

WARNING!

This is not a traditional essay. These pages touch on many different facets of personal game making that you may explore. From time to time you'll be asked to make a choice: what you choose will determine what subjects the essay will explore, and in what order.

Here is an example choice:

To engage with the text as designed, turn to 1 and continue following instructions.

To ignore this aspect of the work and experience it as a linear essay, just continue reading and ignore all further instructions.

---

1 I started a journal shortly after I broke up with my partner of five years. I bought it in an art supply store and hodge-podged a pretty piece of fabric to the cover—circles of color in great looping spirals like a swirl of planetoids.

The journal was part of compact I made with myself to get better at self-care, to give my feelings the space they never got in the five years I had spent supporting another person economically and emotionally. It was also a little reclamation of the girlhood I had been denied when I was an actual kid, an attempt to make up for all the *Dear Diaries* I never got to write.

For several years the bedroom I'd shared with my now-ex was a mess, trash in the corners and clothes covering the floor. You couldn't even see the carpet. Cleaning that room was the first great project I undertook after my breakup. I put a desk in, taped pictures of new lovers to the walls, and scribbled in my journal, safe in the teen-witch bedroom I never had. I lit candles sometimes.

It was the first I'd written with a real pencil on real paper in years. My hand would always hurt by the bottom of a page. So I decided I'd write a page a day. It was hard to fill the space, but it was harder to allow myself not to. It was hard to write every day, but harder not to make myself do it.

I approached it almost the same way I had approached my first Twine game.

If you don't know what Twine is, turn to 2.

To hear about my first Twine game, turn to 3.

2   Twine is a program Chris Klimas wrote in 2009 (a reimpli-
    mentation of an earlier tool, Twee). It's for writing hypertext
stories—stories that use hyperlinks, like websites, to connect
different pages, images, pieces of information. Chris used Twine
to make a few of his own stories—some fictional, some autobiographical—then he threw the program onto the Internet, and
one did very much with Twine for a few years.

I found it while I was looking for something to make *Choose
Your Own Adventure*-style games, those being the branching
Young Adult novels I was obsessed with as a kid. *The thief is
getting away! If you trail him to his hideout, turn to page 53! If
you decide to leave the matter up to the police, turn to page 14.*
(*Choose Your Own Adventure* books were good early reminders:
never trust the police with community matters.)

I sampled a handful of programs, but I ended up using Twine
for a couple reasons: first, it was the simplest. Second, it published finished stories as HTML files, as websites, which seemed
like the most obvious and most radical solution to distributing
games I'd ever seen.

Twine looks like a flowchart on the inside, a bunch of boxes
with arrows pointing to other boxes. Each box is a passage, a page
in a story. You click on a box to give it a name (like "Spiders")
and write in it. To create a link to another passage, you just type
something like:

[[a box full of spiders|Spiders]]

The text on the left is the text the player sees, the word on the right is the name of the passage the player sees when she clicks on it.

If you're still not sure what a _Choose Your Own Adventure_ story is like, reread this essay, following all instructions.

To download Twine, visit twinery.org.

If you're curious why Twine ended up becoming so popular, turn to 4.

To hear about my early experiences with Twine, turn to 3.

---

3 _Encyclopedia Fuckme and the Case of the Vanishing Entree_ wasn't the first Twine game I ever made, but it was the first Twine game I made that got much attention; it was probably the first game that ever got Twine much attention.

I wrote it like a _Choose Your Own Adventure_ book. Almost every passage was a full "page" of text, ending with a choice between two different options. _Encyclopedia Fuckme_ is a porn game about being chased around an apartment by your cannibal girlfriend. I sort of met someone I dated because of it.

It was hard to write complete "pages" of text for almost every moment in the game, but it was harder to allow myself to accept that hypertext living on the web could be as long, or short, and as varied as I could imagine.

To play *Encyclopedia Fuckme and the Case of the Vanishing Entree*, visit http://www.auntiepixelante.com/encyclopediafuckme/

To understand the versatility a hyperlink has, imagine reading this essay in a browser. Clicking on the above url instantly makes the game in question appear. The example is no longer an abstract one. Every hyperlink in a Twine story is like that: it could go to another passage in the story, or to a Twitter conversation, a reference article, an image search, or another Twine story.

If you're curious about how Twine became so popular, turn to 4.

To read about some of the neat ways people have stretched Twine, turn to 5.

---

4 Why did Twine become such a popular game-making tool, especially among marginalized folks and outsiders in games culture?

For one thing, it's free.

It's also, and this can't be overemphasized, Not Programming. People who work in games—who code or who interact with code regularly as part of their job—underestimate just how much of a barrier coding can be. Most people who code have gone to school for years to learn how.

All you need to know to make a game in Twine is how to write. And the same way that people who don't think of themselves as artists know how to doodle on napkins, folks who don't think of themselves as writers know how to scrawl in a journal.

I've done workshops where I've taught little kids and their mothers to make Twine games together. I've given classes to rooms full of queers. I've taught older people to make their first game.

So Twine's more accessible to create with, yes, but its games are also more accessible to play. One of the reasons games can be so alienating is that most of them require you to have grown up holding a controller, and the controllers now all have six buttons, four shoulder triggers, two 360-degree control sticks, and additional hidden buttons when you click the sticks in. Even the simplest indie platformer still relies on manual dexterity in a way that is inaccessible to many people.

Twine games are played with just a mouse and web browser. They don't require dedicated, expensive game consoles. And they don't require more manual skill than what's required to move a mouse and click on links, like any other page on the web. They don't rely on dexterity or time pressure.

Usually.

To hear about my early experiences
working with Twine, turn to 3.

To hear about less traditional things people
have done with Twine, turn to 5.

5 Near the end of 2012, I played a Twine game called *Panic!*
It was written by Astrid Bin and contained code written by
Stefano Russo.

Code? Yeah! Since Twine games are just HTML files—web pages—
they'll run HTML, Javascript, CSS. It's easy to use CSS stylesheets to
change colors, fonts, and transition styles. It's not a lot harder, if you
know how, to use Javascript to create entirely new additions to Twine.

Panic! is a game about escaping from a burning building—there's a timer in the corner that ticks down six seconds,
millisecond by millisecond. In each passage of the game, you
have six seconds to make a decision do you try to escape
through that vent, or do you take your chances in another room?

It's really effective—it's easy to click on things at random, but
what the timer does is make you choose between trying to parse
the text just enough to make an informed decision and clicking on
one of the choices while you still can. You feel panicked, for sure.

They made the game for a game jam in Berlin—that's when a
group of people get together to be in the same space and collaborate on little games. Russo released the source code to the timer
so that anyone could use it. I immediately downloaded it and
then forgot, having no project to use it for. For a while, anyway.

To play *Panic!*, visit http://astridbin.com/
games/panic.html

To download Russo's Twine Timer extension,
visit http://www.glorioustrainwrecks.com/
files/Timer%20Test.tws

If you're skeptical that privileging technical
ingenuity and prowess in yet another sphere
of game making—especially one founded in
simplicity and accessibility—is really such a
good thing, turn to 6.

To hear what I ended up using the timer
code for, turn to 7.

6 I've been extremely wary of extending Twine in showy ways.
I want Twine to continue to be a welcoming space for people
who have little or no knowledge of code. I want people to feel
like it's their voice, not their technical ability, that will be valued.
Modding Twine with Javascript is an option that's only really
available to people who already know their way around code.

I don't think it helps that straight out of the box—without
any CSS modifications—all Twine games have the same white-
on-black design of Twine's Sugarcane story format. Philome.la,
a free website for hosting Twine stories, receives a pile of those
every week. A single CSS tweak—changing the background
color or making the text size bigger—helps set a game apart in
a real way.

Even that single CSS tweak is beyond most people who have never done any kind of web development or coding. I have to look up CSS reference material again every time I write a new Twine story, since CSS is sloppy, full of contradictions, and hard for me to remember.

Chris Klimas and I have talked about making that process easier in the upcoming Twine 2 to allow creators to tweak the apperance of their games without needing to know CSS.

I've kept my games so close to the *Choose Your Own Adventure* format for fear that using technically showy things in my games could make beginners feel pressured to write games that are more technically or visually impressive. For a long time, the most technically impressive Twine game I'd made was *And the Robot Horse You Rode in On*, and all that tweak did was change the background image sometimes.

But then I made *Queers in Love at the End of the World*.

To learn more about Twine's built-in formatting, visit http://twinery.org/wiki/

To read about *Queers in Love*, turn to 7.

---

7 It was another game jam—another one I didn't participate in—that made me realize what I wanted to do with that code. The jam was Ludum Dare—a themed forty-eight-hour game jam that takes place three times a year. This one was the twenty-seventh. The theme was "ten seconds."

Over two thousand ten-second-long games were turned in. I probably played less than one percent of them. I remember a lot of: "Can you save the day in ten seconds?" and "How high can you score in ten seconds?"

What was the hardest thing I could think of to do in ten seconds? The hardest thing I've ever had to do in years of relationships—whether long-distance or under the duress of having no money and trying to tread water—was saying goodbye to my lover. My relationships have always been under time pressure.

That would be the game: in ten seconds, the world is going to end. How's not important. You have ten seconds to say goodbye to your partner, what do you do?

It would be a game of short, sprawling choices: do you tell her you love her, hug her, kiss her? How do you kiss her? There could be as many branches as I could think of. Short passages like heartbeats or exhalations of breath. Some hurried, some lingering. Nothing the same length. Hypertext isn't a book and passages aren't pages. This would be a forest of branches, a thick wood, and on fire.

I started writing this game. It's a good thing I hadn't been in the Ludum Dare competition: after forty-eight hours I was still writing branches for what happens if you want to hold her hand.

Less than a week after I started the game, I broke up with my partner.

If you need to know what happened to *Queers In Love,* turn to 12.

**If you're curious about how the breakup
changed my life, turn to 8.**

---

8 I had spent years supporting other people with my
income—and with my income, that was very, very hard. I
had panic attacks. There were many months I had no idea where
the rent was going to come from. Money—or the scarcity of
it—hung over my head like the sword of Damocles. After my
breakup, one of the first things I needed to do was redecorate:
put away the sword, so I could breathe.

Let's talk about money. Turn to 10.

**If you'd prefer not to talk about
money, turn to 9.**

---

9 Oh, everyone hates having the money conversation. That's
because it's actually a class conversation. Tech culture is
invested in the capitalist idea of a meritocracy—that is, everyone who is successful is successful purely on the value of their
ideas and contributions. Therefore, ANYONE should be able
to succeed, providing they work hard enough or they're smart
enough.

This image ignores that there are a lot of institutionalized
factors that privilege some people over others. Programming
is hard—to be good at it requires years of study and training,

which means engineering school. School is expensive: accessible only to those who have the money to afford it.

Women, who are expected to do a "second shift" as home-makers, rarely have the time to devote to a "hacking" culture that demands hours and hours of unpaid overtime. Most women do plenty of unpaid work already. Queer youth and youth of color are disproportionately expelled from school or are sent to disciplinary alternative schools, and from there they are unlikely to have any chance at higher education.

Don't think the same's not true of the professional world either. In 2013, tech developer Adria Richards, a black woman, lost her job after reporting a sexist joke at a tech conference.

The result is that most of the upper echelons of the tech industry's "meritocracy" are filled with white men. But the indie game scene—which nominally exists in opposition to that corporate establishment—is just as homogenous, and so the dudes who make up what's supposedly a meritocracy are super resistant to acknowledging the privileges that they have. (The same is true of "radical" communities and lots of other spaces.)

The money conversation is hard but important. We use this archetype of the starving artist—the romantic notion that true art comes from poverty, or at least has higher ideals than mere money—to excuse the ways capitalism takes advantage of artists' labor. The game industry has gotten thousands of hours of unpaid "crunch" overtime hours out of game developers by appealing to their "passion" for games.

That carries over to indie and outsider game production as well. If you were really in it for the art, you'd make your games available for free. If people have to pay for them, not only is your art less pure, it's less accessible! What about people who can't afford to pay two dollars for a Twine game?

As silly as this sounds, I bought into this for a long time.

To learn more about the school-to-prison pipeline, visit http://safequalityschools.org/ pages/school-to-prison-pipeline-in-action

To learn about how I finally started making money off my games, turn to 11.

---

10 Part of my self-care pact was finding ways to actually make money off my games. I had done so much unpaid labor for the games community, including releasing every single one of my games for free. I had managed to get some of them sponsored before the Flash bubble burst. The last Flash game I sold, the covered-in-real-newspapers darling *Dys4ia*, made three thousand dollars total—which at the time was a couple months' rent in the Bay Area. I had spent six months making it.

At the Indiecade festival in LA, 2013, I was talking with A Famous Indie Dude. "You don't think people would pay for something like *Dys4ia*?" he asked.

"Maybe now," I shrugged. "But the market was different when the game came out."

"He's right, you know," merritt kopas said to me later that day. "You need to ask for more money for your games, because people will pay for them."

I was experimenting with putting a Twine game up for sale after I got back from LA. I was going to charge a dollar, plus an optional additional donation.

"Make it two," she said.

I promised her I would sell my game for two dollars if she did the same with her game—which ended up being *Consensual Torture Simulator*. They both ended up doing really well, better than either of us expected, I think.

**If you want to know how I made money
off of *Queers in Love*, turn to 11.**

**If you're more interested in how I wrote
the game, turn to 12.**

---

11 So I had a little store on Gumroad—a site that's more often used to sell comics—with a couple of games in it. I didn't put every game I made up for sale. I still wanted to be able to make all the little, free-to-play projects that I felt were too small or too neat to sell, but that I nevertheless spent a nontrivial amount of time and energy on. I still needed to make some money on those. So I set up a Patreon account.

Here's how Patreon works: people pledge me a certain amount of money per game. Once a month, I release a game that's free to play, and I receive the total amount of money people have pledged. (I have one "incentive" for big spenders: if you pledge at least twenty-five dollars per game, I will whisper your name in a lover's ear.)

The problem with Patreon—and Kickstarter, and crowd-funding in general—is that mostly what it accomplishes is to recirculate money within marginalized communities. It's mostly other queer people who make slightly more than me who are paying me every month. Crowdfunding rarely brings in the money of those who actually have it, the kind of wealth that gets spent on TED Talk presenters. It's a temporary solution.

The first game I'm going to release for my Patreon, I told myself, will be *Queers in Love at the End of the World*. It wasn't. Part of my self-care was realizing I couldn't finish it by the end of the month, so I made something else instead of binge-working to finish it on time. The first game I released, in October, was a Twine game about long-distance relationships.

To play *I Summon You*, a Twine game
about long-distance relationships, visit
http://auntiepixelante.com/isummonyou/

If you'd rather hear about how *Queers in
Love* got finished, turn to 12.

---

12 *In her eyes, you are you, the way you really are, not the way you see yourself when you look into the mirror, your face and body distorted by learned self-hatred. The real you.*
I finished *Queers in Love at the End of the World* in November 2013. The game tries to seem overwhelming in size—the first passage has four links and those four passages each have a

bunch more. Gradually the branches narrow, eventually arriving at some kind of dead end—a long block of descriptive text, a chain of linear passages, or an endless loop. Within the ten-second time limit, you never notice the artifice, or you're out of time anyway.

It was still a lot of writing. And as I doggedly filled out what ended up being over 180 unique passages, I started drawing heavily on my personal experiences. I wrote about being a trans woman in a world that systemically challenges my identity, and the affirmation I find in a partner's admiration. I wrote about my fears of the police state, how society tries to keep us divided, the connections we make anyway, torches in the night, and how we keep them burning.

I wrote from the experience of relationships with people who couldn't always be around, and who couldn't always afford to be present in a material way. I wrote from the experience of relationships that had ended, knowing the importance of those times and spaces in my life, even though they had burned out. There was a time limit with those I loved. There was always a return flight home, a threat of eviction, or money and resources—always too few—running out. There was never enough time.

I was thirty and in the throes of a breakup when I made *Queers in Love*. Mortality and possibility were twin horns rising on either side of me. I wanted to make a game about the transcendant power of what I shared with my lovers—support, grounding, criminal collusion—even if my time with them was too short.

Those Twine passages were like journal pages, and like journal pages I filled them—sometimes with a single sentence, sometimes with a single word. Maybe that's why Twine is so popular: every passage is just a blank page, asking for nothing more or less important than your thoughts, your dreams, your experiences.

Letters tossed from a burning building.

If you're interested in how queer authors have repurposed the post-apocalyptic setting, turn to 13.

If you're more interested in why someone would choose a game as the format for a personal story at all, turn to 14.

---

13 You used to hike out to the landfill, sit on a cliff looking over the formless sea, and let yourself imagine that civilization was finally over, the wheels of empire ground to a halt, the truncheons dropped where they were lifted.

The post-apocalypse, in popular culture, often represents a macho libertarian fantasy. There's no government! Finally, we can break out the family guns. What's the appeal of the now-prolific "zombie apocalypse" genre other than that it provides a backdrop against which Ordinary Americans can justify shooting tons and tons of people?

For marginalized people, though—and this is me speaking as

15 In the aftermath of a string of poly breakups, I wonder whether it's good to claim so much validation from partners. I haven't been single in years: I've always been in enough overlapping relationships that whenever I break up with one partner, there are others to comfort me. What would it be like to be single again? Where would my validation come from then?

I try—when I can—to see these breakups as opportunities for self-care, as reaffirmations of my ability to support myself and to stand on my own legs. Maybe I owe my partners as much for that as for anything else they've given me.

Queers in Love at the End of the World stands as a kind of journal entry from a time of transition in my life—aren't they all, though?—when I was examining what it was that I took from love and partnership. All journals will be cinders when the world burns, and all Twine games unplayable when the cables go offline and the Internet finally sleeps.

But the truth is the world is always on fire. And these moments are still real.

**To play *Queers in Love at the End of the World*,
visit http://auntiepixelante.com/endoftheworld/**

**For my full tutorial on making games in Twine,
visit http://auntiepixelante.com/twine/**

Now, write your own.

You spent a lifetime sending out signals you were scared would be misinterpreted, misunderstood, garbled, absorbed, allowed to pass unregistered into the cold of space.

Now you know.

The signal was never lost.

anna anthropy is a video game designer, author, and creator of games such as Lesbian Spider Queens of Mars *and* Queers In Love at the End of the World. *Her first book,* Rise of the Videogame Zinesters, *was published in 2012 by Seven Stories Press. Part manifesto and part manual, it makes the case for games as means for self-expression and political activism.*

The Natural:
The Parameters of Afro

EVAN NARCISSE

As the video game industry continues to strive for photorealistic graphics and lifelike human characters, while simultaneously taking on real-world or historical settings, it is inescapably confronted with its own prejudices and stereotypes. In this essay, Evan Narcisse examines the relationship—or lack thereof—between the video game industry and black culture, putting a spotlight on how game developers tackle and fail to tackle subjects such as slavery and racism.

EVERY MORNING AFTER I WAKE UP, I RUN A PICK THROUGH my hair. It's important that I do this when my hair is still spongy and damp from the shower. Wait too long and it gets more dry and less cooperative, making it harder to pull the comb through my natural. (Pro tip: A natural is something black folks sometimes call hair that hasn't been altered or straightened by heat or chemicals.)

After the picking out, patting down, and shaping are done, I always think to myself, "Goddamn, I love being black."

Video games have yet to deliver the same feeling to me.

My hair doesn't really qualify as an Afro or even a baby Afro. It's kind of a dark taper fade, with the sides grown out a bit. It's exactly the kind of haircut that millions of black men all over the world have been wearing for centuries. Millennia, even. And yet it remains exactly the kind of detail that the science-fiction wizardry of modern-day game making hasn't figured out how to replicate.

When you see the billboards and TV commercials for big-budget video games out in the world, it can feel like the designers and programmers in the game business are just a few algorithms away from breathing life into eerily accurate human avatars. The days of a neckless Mario or a Link with unarticulated fingers are long gone. Lots of modern games let you craft your own hero, opening up the rendering power of its software to the player. That's within certain parameters, of course. When a game lets me create a character to be a protagonist, the first thing I try to do is recreate myself in digital form. It's an uncontrollable urge, a kneejerk reflex borne from decades of never seeing enough black people—ones who weren't tokens, punchlines, or subhuman caricatures—inside the comics, TV shows, movies, and, yes, video games I took in while growing up.

The create-a-character options in video games like *Mass Effect*, *Skyrim*, or *Destiny* can be marvelous things. They have on-screen tools and visual effects options that let you control how far apart your avatar's eyes are or the length of the bridge of his nose. I can reproduce my thick lips or wide nose sometimes. A goatee? No problem. But when it comes to head hair—specifically locks that look like what grows from my scalp—I'm generally out of luck.

Not all black hairstyles are so neglected. Big, blown-out Afros or high-top fades get thrown out there from time to time, often to comedic effect. When Allen Iverson and urban gangsta flicks like *Menace II Society* captured the imagination of white folks worldwide, you'd see characters with cornrows or long braids in video games. Likewise, dreadlocks tend to be a staple of black video game hairstyles now. Cornrows and dreadlocks have some things in common. They can approximate the way that white hair generally grows: down past the ears and shoulders. Hell, straight on down to the back, if the wearer feels footloose and fancy free. But, the other thing the two styles have in common is the whiff of fad or trend. Dreadlocks and cornrows went from being controversial styles that a small segment of the population wore to ones that became more acceptable to society at large, and they remain heavily exoticized.

Both inside and outside black communities, these two styles took on meanings. Inside black communities, cornrows often get worn for their ease of care and dreadlocks can be meant to symbolize religious convictions and/or ethnic pride. But outside black communities, people wearing these styles have been subject to cultural discrimination, with schools and employers refusing to admit students or to hire workers who wear them. Progressive changes in perception have happened in large part because of cultural movers like Bob Marley or Allen Iverson. Dreadlocks and cornrows gradually became part of a visual shorthand that communicated spirituality, edginess, or threat. Afros were controversial once, too, but wound up taking a left turn on the path to mainstreaming. They're now understood in a comedic way—as a style so outlandish that only the truly goofyludicrous would wear it. It's telling that the equivalent for straight hair—locks that go down past the shoulders, say—isn't a signifier of immanent hijinx. Video game producers and art directors put dreadlocks in their creations to draw on that shorthand. "See, our black character is spiritual. Or edgy. Or threatening. Or threateningly edgy in a spiritual way. What's that?! An Afro?! Boy, this black guy must really funny! Get ready to laugh at him, players!" Look at a natural and what do you think? "Boy, that sure is . . . middle of the road."

A hairstyle like mine just grows how it grows. Sure, I get it cut a certain way. But it's still pretty conservative. Boring. Common. Like I said before, millions of black men have been letting their hair grow like mine since time immemorial. Sidney Poitier. Morgan Freeman. Kofi Annan. Nintendo of America's Reggie Fils-Aime. Chiwetel Ejiofor. My dad. The people making video games probably see it a few times a day, even if it's just on TV or the Internet. That's what makes it so puzzling that a good-looking version of the basic natural has proven to be such a rare beast during my travels through hundreds of video games.

Usually, I have to settle. I resign myself to picking the black color option out of a customization palette wheel and selecting a cut that hews relatively close to the scalp. The caesar cuts of myriad video games—like George Clooney used to wear in his early days on E.R.— have become a glum safe-haven for my natural aspirations. "Ok, fine," I tell myself, "I guess I can choke this down. I always wanted to look like a Klingon from the original Star Trek 1960s episodes." (No, not really. I haven't wanted that look. No one ever has.) Another black friend told me, "I've done this exact thing so many times. It's this moment in online games, when I'm on a Skype call with my friends waiting for me to join them. I just sorta break down and go, ugh, fine, the caesar is close enough." Even when I lie to myself and say that the color and density are close to acceptable, I can still see the stringy, thread-like locks fringing around the hairline. Nope. Not black hair. At least, it's not my black hair.

It's the visual texture that's the trickiest part, I'd imagine. From afar, hair like mine looks like a solid, unified dome. But, it's actually a particulate mass, made of hyper-tight curls that pretty much resist gravity by growing up and out. There's a chunk on the left side of my head that grows faster and thicker than the right side. I've got to pat it down more. Sometimes, it sticks out more stubbornly and destroys any fantasies I have of rocking a symmetrical ebony corona. In photographs with strong lighting, you can make out the wooly piles of waves where the uniformity has broken back down into unruly almost-tendrils. I understand the challenge in recreating this tonsorial paradox—unified yet individuated, cottony yet coarse—in the virtual visuals of video games.

So, what then? What will it take to perfect the video game natural? Better processing chips for the graphics cards living inside the computers and game consoles? Bleeding-edge software engines to create the digital worlds and individuals of future games? Both of those inevitabilities would be good starts. But, honestly, that stuff already happens on a cyclical basis. Computing power and coding prowess march along in lockstep with each other, destined to further enable the imaginations of the people using them. It's the human imagination that is the game maker's most important tool. And that's why the birth of the one true video game natural needs one thing. Most simply, there needs to be more black people making video games.

Any conversation about black hair is, at its roots, about more than the follicles growing on a given body. These talks are really about the intersection of personal choice and inherited standards, the crossroads where we decide what products and treatments we're going to use to give our hair certain looks. Video games get steam from the friction generated at that crossroads. People who choose to make games or who identify as gamers have historically rubbed up against cultural snobbery and moral panics, the result of standards that dismiss games as mere commerce. Activists like disbarred anti-gaming gadfly lawyer Jack Thompson, or disgraced California lawmaker Leland Yee have tried to influence popular opinion and jurisprudence in ways that essentially would have had games treated as radioactive, world-destroying material. Mainstream media reports about violent video games whip the non-playing public into a frenzy about the evils that video games might be wreaking on our minds. (You, dear reader, might even be one of those snobs or panickers!) So it makes sense that video game creators and enthusiasts like to trumpet their favorite medium's accomplishments. Some cheerleaders will sing hosannas for the groundbreaking nature of digital interactivity, the core difference that generates a sense of immersion that makes games different from movies or books. Others will invoke a record-breaking 24-hour sales number like the kind notched by *Grand Theft Auto V* or *Call of Duty: Ghosts* as a sign that video games are equivalent to or better than the other media they out-earn. Video games are a smart, forward-looking art form, triumphalists say, one that uses its seductive interactivity to absorb, re-present, and re-contextualize all that has come before it. Resistance is futile, non-players.

But bring up the medium's shortcomings and you often get flustered defensiveness in response. One of those shortcomings is in the lack of diversity of the people who are making and are portrayed in video games.

The modern era of video games—let's call it the last twenty years or so—has barely seen any black lead characters in big-budget or independent small-team video games. Oh, there've been sidekicks and boon companions aplenty. Too many of those have relied on tropes and stereotypes that are embarrassingly retrograde. There's been *Dead Island*'s Sam B., a street-tough, one-hit-wonder rapper whose single was, "Who Do You Voodoo, Bitch." *Deus Ex: Human Revolution* had Letitia, an indigent woman on the streets of a dystopian sci-fi future Detroit who somehow sounded like she came off the set of the cheesy 1970s cop drama *Starsky & Hutch*. And a whole parade of hot-tempered brawn-centric bruisers and slangtastic slicksters have appeared in fighting game series like *Street Fighter* and *King of Fighters*, with names like Heavy D!, TJ Combo, and Dee Jay, all clearly meant to convey a hip urban lifestyle in the broadest of strokes. And there've been dozens, maybe hundreds of other lesser lights (lesser darknesses?) in the deluge of store-bought and digitally downloaded games: men assembled in thrall to gritty hollow machismo, and women constructed to deliver trite sass or lurid titillation. Each one of them burdened with the weight of expectations they can't possibly fulfill, because for every character like them, thousands of non-black characters get more spotlight and more chance for nuance.

Where are the games starring a main guy or gal—the buck-stops-here character entrusted with anchoring empathy, narrative, and design ambition—who is a black person? There are all too few. My quest to find and wear the natural I want might not be quite as quixotic if there were games with black protagonists. Mind you, there has been fitful progress in the last few years. In particular, the *Assassin's Creed* series from French publisher Ubisoft has found intriguing story and gameplay ideas in the ways that black people have defied oppressive systems throughout history. The main conceit of the *Assassin's Creed* games is that they send players to sumptuously recreated cities of centuries past, plopping them in pivotal moments like the Crusades or the Renaissance and letting them encounter luminaries like Leonardo DaVinci. Amidst free-running acrobatics, lurking-in-shadows stealth, and swordplay and gunplay combat, the games in the series have had aspirations of imparting a sense of the political and cultural upheaval of the time periods they're set in.

Ubisoft has released two *Assassin's Creed* games with black lead characters set during the height of the 18th Century transatlantic slave trade. *Assassin's Creed: Liberation* featured Aveline de Granpre, a bi-racial heroine whose French father once owned her black mother. Set in the New Orleans of 1768, Aveline's adventures find her investigating the whereabouts of vanished slaves and searching for her own long-lost mother Jeanne. The character's special abilities let her don three separate guises, each with its own strengths. As a high-society Lady, she can bribe officials for access to closed-off areas. She can cause riots while wearing the tattered rags of the Slave. Her third persona, the Assassin, lets her do much of what other lead characters in the series can do, like killing with a hidden blade and using pistols. This game mechanic of switching roles plays off of her bi-racial background, all in the midst of a game set during a time when black people were little more than property. She's of two worlds and has abilities that let her move through them.

Players can discover pages from Aveline's mother's diary in *Liberation*. As you collect them, you see her command of the written word increase as she learns to read and write in secret defiance of the real-life laws that denied slaves the power of literacy. Collectible items like this are a well-trod element in many video games, but the historical insight woven into the mechanic here creates unexpected poignancy. You don't see it happen, but reading the diary pages lets players feel Jeanne transform from someone else's property into her own person.

More than a year after *Liberation*'s release, *Assassin's Creed: Freedom Cry* came out as a downloadable add-on for *Assassin's Creed IV: Black Flag*. The main game featured pirate hero Edward Kenway seeking his fortune while dodging the armadas of the French, Spanish, and British. His first mate, Adewale, was a former slave who kept Kenway's crew in line and his vessel seaworthy. The *Freedom Cry* add-on focused on Adewale decades after his time with Kenway, with a ship and crew of his own.

Adewale's time on the roiling seas of the Caribbean wasn't about getting rich, though. After a fateful ship battle leaves him stranded on Saint Domingue—the island that's home to the countries now known as Haiti and the Dominican Republic— players controlled him as he sought to liberate slaves and help foment uprisings. I'm a Haitian-American child of immigrants and, personally, *Freedom Cry* felt like a deeply resonant fictional telling of the history my ancestors came from. Hearing passersby discuss the sub-humanity of slaves doing backbreaking labor, or giving chase to slave catchers pursuing runaways trying to escape to freedom gave me motivations I had never felt before playing video games. One of *Freedom Cry*'s last sections takes place in a sinking slave ship, with Adewale trying to escape a watery grave. All the while, you're surrounded by hundreds of kidnapped Africans you know you won't be able to save.

Those *Assassin's Creed* games tap into the historical circumstances of black people in the Western world for inspiration. But another recent game did none of that and still delivered an interesting character. *Remember Me*, a sci-fi video game much like the hit British cop drama *Luther*, is meaningful because it's not a protest document centered on race. The blackness of their lead characters is incidental. These characters don't serve as signifiers for any attitudes in their fictional universe. Detective Chief Inspector Luther isn't tortured because of racism; he's tortured because he walks the line between legal punishment of serial killer horrors and the temptation of outside-the-law vengeance. In *Remember Me*, Nilin is a memory hunter, a special operative who invades the psyches of targets to reshape or eliminate remembrances. She doesn't manipulate people's memories because she's descended from a people who've suffered horrific erasures. Her motivation for being a memory hunter comes from her family history, not her racial background in particular. By their mere presence and well-executed dramatic arcs, she and John Luther make for strong evolutionary leaps in the portrayal of black characters in their respective media.

Lee Everett didn't have a great natural. You can tell that he's supposed to, but it . . . it's just not right. Nevertheless, the lead character of the first season of a series of games based on *The Walking Dead* is one of the best black personas ever created for a game. Though he was an escaped ex-con, Lee's soulful regret and concern for a little girl named Clementine humanized him out of the bounds of any facile stereotype. He wasn't quick to violence or emotionally inarticulate. Indeed, the very nature of the game had players steering Lee through an uneasy leadership of zombie apocalypse survivors, with agonizing life-or-death decisions at every turn. He was more empathetic and well-rounded than most other game protagonists, whether black or white. He never felt like an exoticized curiosity. With a few horrifically bad decisions and waves of undead swarming all over me, he felt like someone I could be.

In the *Assassin's Creed* games, Aveline and Adewale's motivations come in direct response to historical racial oppressions they lived under. Luther and Nilin represent another strategy of creating a black character for popular consumption, where race never gets explicitly addressed. They're black but not centered by any definition of blackness. The strategy is more subtle in Lee Everett's particular character construction in *The Walking Dead*. The institutions that have historically doled out prejudice have largely crumbled in the game's undead-infested world, but Lee is still imagined in the context of blackness in the American south. The game's characters mostly hail from Atlanta, and Lee engages with folks who have different sorts of beliefs about him because of his blackness. Fellow survivor Kenny thinks that he can pick locks "because he's urban." Another character distrusts Lee's potential romantic involvement with his daughter. It's never explicitly tied to race, but the echoes of interracial romance dramas like *Guess Who's Coming to Dinner* can still be felt in these scenes. And the there's the question of Lee's young charge Clementine. They're both brown, which leaves some folks unable to tell if they're biologically related or not, regardless of whether they actually look like father and daughter.

The most hopeful thing about Lee, Nilin, Aveline, and Adewale is that they all come across as different from each other and from what's come before. If video games are really to be the prime creative vessel of the coming century, then there should be room for blackness—or, more aptly, for the myriad forms of it—inside of the medium. We don't need the haircuts and poses that communicate a fascination with "the Other"—"Let's spice up our game with a brown-colored person!"—but ones that reflect an understanding of what it's like to be a regular black person. It's reasonable to want more of each strategy mentioned above: games that directly address race as central, games that treat race as purely aesthetic, or at least don't address it in the text, allowing audiences to draw their own conclusions, and games that address race but don't make it central. This is how the skeleton of a continuum of portrayals can get built. Right now, our skeleton has a clavicle and a tailbone, maybe, but nothing capable of supporting much weight.

A few years ago, I wrote about my frustrations on the popular video game culture website Kotaku. I called my article, "Come On, Video Games, Let's See Some Black People I'm Not Embarrassed By," and the main thesis was about how the medium needs to tap into the phenomenon of Black Cool. This is part of what I wrote:

What I want, basically, is Black Cool. It's a kind of cool that improvises around all the random stereotypes and facile understandings of black people that have accrued over centuries and subverts them. Black Cool says, "I know what you might think about me, but I'm going to flip it." Dave Chappelle's comedy is Black Cool. Donald Glover is Black Cool. Aisha Tyler is Black Cool. Marvel Comics's Black Panther character is Black Cool. Their creativity is the energy I want video games to tap into.

And more:

In other mediums and creative pursuits, there've been the black people who pivoted the conversations, expanded the possibilities and deepened the portrayals about what black people are. In jazz, it was Charlie Parker. In literature, it was Ralph Ellison. In comics, I'd argue that it was Christopher Priest, followed by Dwayne McDuffie. For me, the work of the deceased McDuffie managed to create characters that communicated an easily approachable vein of Black Cool.

Video games need this kind of paradigm-shifting figure. Not an exec, mind you—sorry, Reggie—but a creative face who steers the ethos of a game. For example, you know what kind of game a Warren Spector or a Jenova Chen is going to deliver. With Spector, it's a game that'll spawn consequences from player action. With Chen, you'll get experiences that try to expand the emotional palette of the video game medium. I want someone to carry that flag for blackness, to tap into it as a well of ideas.

Since then, I occasionally get responses from people who've read the article, asking if such-and-such character from Video Game X passes muster. "He's not so bad," the yearning goes. But there's an addendum I haven't written for that years-old essay, which is that Black Cool isn't enough.

Black Cool isn't an end, understand; it's a means to one. It's a coping mechanism for existing in a world that's denigrated and dehumanized you. It's a way to freeze off the small slights and mega-disenfranchisements. You can break them off to keep on keeping on, but doing so still breaks off a little flesh with it, like freezing off a wart.

Black Cool is a response to being denied a more complete humanity. "Choose not to acknowledge me in my fullness?" it asks "Then all you get is the chill." The thing that too often goes unsaid is that Black Cool is cold comfort for the practitioner, too. It doesn't make up for lost opportunities. If you're cool and broke, you're still broke. If you're cool and two-dimensional, you're just a different kind of caricature.

For all the progress of late, I've grown tired of playing video games with black characters that feel they were brokered into existence. My eyes can pick out the seams of compromise as I play through them: the not-good-enough hair, the broken speech patterns, the trope-laden backstories.

I've heard firsthand from both black and white video game designers who've had to walk their corporate employers back from the cliff's edge of truly rank embarrassment when it comes to crafting tertiary characters of African descent. I've also indirectly heard stories of black marketing and public relations representatives who have tried to warn their higher-ups that the games they were pushing out the door had discomfiting echoes of centuries-old propaganda that portrayed black people as subhuman. Those games went out unchanged. In each case, the black folk involved weren't high enough on the ladder to command the requisite levels of control needed to make substantive changes.

Even black-protagonist video games that I like have their flaws. In *Freedom Cry*, there was the messy stumble where the game's mechanics turned the same slaves you fought to free into currency to get more deadly weapons. It was essentially something like, "Liberate 300 more slaves to get access to this cool machete." Wait, isn't that the same commodification that I just worked to end inside the game's narrative? I played through that and wondered if that blunder would have happened if a majority of the people who worked on the game were black or from other people-of-color backgrounds.

When I think about what excites me about video games and what excites me most about being black, it doesn't seem like such a weird impossibility that the two should intersect. What excites me about video games—at their best anyway— is when the conglomeration of mechanical systems, music, and art congeal into a result that's capable of being deeply expressive about the human experience. A video game like Jason Rohrer's *Passage* can make me melancholy about my own mortality. *Brothers: A Tale of Two Sons*—made by filmmaker Josef Fares and game development studio Starbreeze—is a playable fable about the strengths we get from siblings, life partners, or other meaningful relationships.

What excites me about being black is being connected to a history of resistance, innovation, and improvisation—a history extruded out from under the most inhumane physical, psychological, and systemic oppressions in human history. Ralph Ellison's *Invisible Man* is only trenchant, angry, and darkly funny because it rebelliously gives voice to an existence that defied all the forces that tried to suppress it. Of course, I don't have to live inside any of that understanding if I don't want to. I can take from it as I want or need. Canadian poet Dionne Brand once remarked that, "To live in the Black diaspora is I think to live as a fiction—a creation of empires, & also self-creation."

Yes, the empires of the video game landscape—big publishers like EA, Ubisoft, and Activision—are making their slow, stumbly tentative progress. But it's really the self-creation of black video game characters and universes that I hold out the most hope for.

When I initiated a series of back-and-forth letters about black people and video games on Kotaku, my correspondent David Brothers and I talked about *Blazing Saddles*, the classically impolite cowboy comedy by Mel Brooks, about a black sheriff in the Old West. An embrace of satire would help game makers work touchy subjects like race into their games, I argued:

> . . . People don't want to be taken the wrong way, especially if they want to make games that somehow touch on race.
>
> That's why satire—with its ability to lower defense mechanisms with laughter—seems like a much

more attractive option. What I really want is a video game equivalent to *Blazing Saddles*. Mel Brooks' classic western comedy hones in on the anxieties of its time—a post-segregation moment when black and white people are still warily integrating in various social spheres—to fuel its jokes. There are tropes in black arts traditions that game designers can use, too. Cleavon Little's sheriff in *Blazing Saddles* has a bit of the trickster in him; he reorders society by going against the grain. The whole movie runs up and tongue kisses every stereotype it can find. It's entirely possible that people watching might use the stereotypes to reinforce really nasty worldviews, but that's clearly not the film's aim.

And, yeah, *Blazing Saddles* is absurd slapstick. But so is the root of most prejudices, right?

I want a game that pokes fun at the fact that 99.9% of game protagonists look like cousins. I want a game that clowns the thinking that noble savages are still a good plot point in 2012. I want a game that doesn't feel the need to turn its black characters into thuggish stereotypes just because it's an easy shorthand for being a bad-ass.

Brothers responded:

Here's something else to think about: You mention *Blazing Saddles* being a good goal-setter for games. I agree, and would actually include *Friday*, the near-perfect 1995 film starring Ice Cube and Chris Tucker, in that category. But *Blazing Saddles* had Cleavon Little in front of the camera, Richard Pryor on the script, and a booming black presence in Hollywood to balance it out. *Friday* had black culture exploding into the mainstream, rap beginning the process of absorbing every other genre, and a string of realistic black condition-type movies like *Rosewood, New Jack City, Boyz n the Hood*, and *Menace II Society* to play off. If you weren't into *Blazing Saddles* or *Friday*, if they offended you or just weren't your bag, you could easily find an alternative.

In video games, those alternatives are almost nonexistent. New York City-based game designer Shawn Allen turned to Kickstarter to crowdfund *Treachery in Beatdown City*, a throw-back action game happening in a rapidly gentrifying analog to Manhattan. The game features a multi-racial trio of heroes and a unique blend of strategy and virtual fisticuffs. There's a sense that this in-development game—whether good or bad—will be the product of the undiluted vision of Allen and his co-creators. The fact that you're beating up wave after wave of thugs to save a black President? That's his decision. Same for the music, art style, and side stories the video game will have. This game won't be focus-tested into blandness.

However, while I'm chomping at the bit for a black grassroots sensibility to spontaneously generate in video games, I'm also conflicted that it will ever come about. In my worst moments, I'm pessimistic that video games will ever experience the emergence of a Black Arts movement analog. Structurally, it seems like the elements that allowed writers, filmmakers, playwrights, and poets to organize around a desire to tell their own black histories, comedies, and tragedies won't ever congeal in a similar way for video games. The small-team indie stratum of modern game making is one of the most exciting sectors of the medium right now. Huge swells of support surround the creators trying to crowdfund their visions into being. But the number of black people in those circles is minimal.

The right mix of patronage, mentorship, and wanton risk-taking doesn't feel manifest right now. Leaving aside any questions about personal and individual courage, the most blatant reality is that diversifying the pool of people who star in and make games is too big a distraction. The profit margins are so thin and the struggle for relevance so fraught that it feels like most captains of industry are constantly trying not to run their vessels aground. So, the pipelines that feed talent into the game-making ecosystem—where, as elsewhere, people hire in their own image and based on social proximity—seem fated to remain homogenous. The would-be black creators never get the chance to start out paying dues in corporate careers that they can then leave to go indie and create more personal visions.

And, if we're honest, there was an element of ego-stroking cultural tourism motivating some of the non-black people who championed black creators in previous decades when institutional racism stymied the entrance of black people into creative professions. I'm talking about people like Carl Van Vechten, the white writer who helped black authors like Langston Hughes get their work put out by big publishing houses during the Harlem

Renaissance—"Look, Beauregard, not only did I venture forth into Deepest Darkest, but I've returned with one that can actually write!" It seems exploitative in hindsight, but that kind of relationship still opened doors that would be otherwise closed. Let's compare it to the world of film. Before, say, Spike Lee directed his first big feature film, some film professor of his had to believe in him enough—or be egotistical enough—to introduce him to the people who would eventually put him in the director's chair. Even that kind of tortured dynamic seems to be missing from the video game business.

Part of this is because there's a stripe of player and creator who want games to be apolitical and ahistorical. They don't understand why it's important that my particular kind of black hair is pretty much missing from video games. We're living in a post-racial meritocracy, no?

If we were really post-racial, then putting a black lead character in a game wouldn't matter, right? Nary a second thought would be given. But every time the issue comes up, it meets an ugly response. I work in a position that lets me see these responses up close, and there's nothing post-racial about them. They're filled with a dismissiveness about the past injustices that black people have borne. They say, "That stuff is in the past, black people. Quit your complaining and make your own video games." Comedian Louis CK famously knocked down and out that mode of thinking on an episode of *The Tonight Show With Jay Leno*, saying: "Every year, white people add a hundred years to how long ago slavery was. I've heard educated white people say that slavery was 400 years ago. No, it very much wasn't. It was a 140 years ago. That's two seventy-year-old ladies living and dying back to back. That's how recently you could buy a guy."

Institutional racism doesn't fall away that quickly, and neither do its various implements and consequences, especially when candid discussion about any of those things is so sparse. It's not as easy as that trollish retort would make it seem. Video games, like all pop culture, exist in an ecosystem. It's a web of interconnected entities that are constantly trying to harness ideas, manpower, and energy for creative and competitive advantage. And, still, the huge untapped black audience ready to see and create themselves in today's games remain an invisible elephant in corporate boardrooms.

Look, I don't like Tyler Perry's movies. But I'm not so blind as to not see that Perry's work as a producer, director, and actor succeeds because he's able to give a starving audience images of themselves—not as growly fetish objects, but as hard-working, church-going folk. You never have to worry about the one black guy in his movies being less than upstanding, because there's never just one black guy. A Tyler Perry movie will have enough black women in it for him to sprinkle different personality traits around. His power and influence come as a result of the simplest supply and demand, power-in-numbers arithmetic in the world. Somehow, that math does not compute to the movers and shakers in the video game business. They'll go with what looks exotic and foreign in their construction of black characters, ignorant all the while of the fact that their potential black audience can see the chicanery from miles away.

In the real world, I tried to rock a different look for a while. My flirtation with a bald head came in college. The rap group Onyx, made up of a cluster of rowdy, hyperactive rappers, was enjoying its short window of popularity then. With a crew of friends, I emulated their clean-shaven pates when "Slam" was all over the airwaves. But putting my scalp on display fell away after a few months. In that particular moment, rocking a baldie may have been what was deemed cool, but it didn't feel like me, not deep down. After all, what was it that had countered the self-consciousness I had felt throughout the years about my narrow, oval head shape and ears that stuck out wide? What was it that the white boys in my Catholic high school tried to insult—without ever understanding—in the showers after gym class? It was my natural.

Call it self-indulgent, but I've come to believe that maintaining a natural is a work of art. Sometimes I compare combing and shaping my hair to sculpting clay. The most important part happens when it's wet, but the shape it takes when dry is all people will see during the course of a given day. I wonder what I keep doing it all for, too. My hairline's receded a damnable amount and there's only so much longer that I'll be able to hide the thinning patches at the top of my head. But, for now, I'm not going to shave it all off. I'm going to keep maintaining my natural in the probably delusional hope that video game creators large and small will learn how to import it—and the humanity lived by people who wear it—into their works.

Evan Narcisse is a journalist and media critic. He writes for Kotaku *and has contributed to* Time Magazine.

What It's Like to Always Play the Bad Guy: On the Portrayal of Arabs in Online Shooters

HUSSEIN IBRAHIM

The image of the Arab as a religious fundamentalist and terrorist is prevalent in all forms of Western pop culture. But nowhere is this more obvious than in video games, in particular military-themed online shooters. Here, you are not simply a passive consumer of entertainment, but an active participant. You are expected to point a rifle at your enemy and to pull the trigger. But what if the enemy is meant to represent your own culture? In this essay, video game journalist Hussein Ibrahim explores what makes him and so many others keep playing these games, and why they remain popular in the Arab world.

WHETHER IT'S THE NEWS, TELEVISION, OR MOVIES, ARABS have become synonymously linked with the word "terrorist." And thanks to video games, we've become the target—literally.

The thing is, we're not alone as targets: the Russians, Chinese, Vietnamese, and Germans all join us, but Arabs have been in the limelight for the last few years. In the limelight, but not as the heroes.

I've been playing games for as long as I remember. Growing up in Detroit in the early '90s put me in the first PlayStation era. Games like *Crash Bandicoot* and *Spyro the Dragon* kept me entertained in my early years.

A few years down the line, my family and I moved from the US to Egypt. My dad worked as a civil engineer and was offered a new job in Cairo. Having never left Detroit, it was the culture clash of a lifetime between two completely different parts of the world with completely different lifestyles. The only thing that really kept me sane were my video games.

As I grew a little older and became more accustomed to the lifestyle there, I started visiting the local LAN center. There, it turned out, everyone played nothing but *Counter Strike*, a shooter game where two teams—one terrorist and one counter-terrorist—compete for dominance on battlefields inspired by real-life locations. That was my first real encounter with a competitive multiplayer game.

Safe to say, it was love at first sight. As a kid, I played almost any game I could get my hands on, but I always had an attraction to online multiplayer games. I loved playing in a room filled with friends, and I felt comforted by the idea that I could always return to that same LAN center and find them there.

I've always liked shooters because there's such a clear element of skill involved. At the LAN center, there was always someone better than me. A game like *Counter Strike* does a great job of highlighting the best player, because skill gaps become hugely apparent while playing. One could, and I would, argue that competitive shooters are the closest thing gaming comes to professional sports.

A few years later, I moved to Beirut, Lebanon, where I still live and work today. I played *Halo* semi-professionally, competing in tournaments, and when I wasn't playing, I was working as an editor for At7addak.com, the leading online video game community in the Middle East.

Most, if not all, competitive online shooters are produced by Western game studios, primarily those based in the US. But they regularly top the sales charts in the Middle East too. As in many other countries across the world, there is a large and thriving competitive shooter scene in Lebanon today. But for us, the experience is a little bit different than it is for you, provided that you are not also from the Middle East.

Let me describe a typical scene from one of the games I play. On my screen, I see a dusty courtyard in a desert landscape. An arm with a gun in hand—my hand—is pointing forward. Suddenly, an emotionally-detached, bearded AI armed with an AK-47, dressed in raggedy clothes and bare feet, comes running out of nowhere and stands in the middle of the courtyard, shooting and yelling in "Arabic." My objective is to kill him.

In most modern games like *Call of Duty* or *Battlefield*, the "Arabic" is actually Arabic. On the other hand, some games don't even try. Check out the this image from *Splinter Cell: Conviction*.

The street sign on the right is actually written in proper Arabic. The sign on the left, however, is just a bunch of squiggly lines. I can't understand why only one sign got the proper treatment.

Other games use proper Arabic but space each letter apart like a separate word. *Call of Duty* correctly uses Arabic in the game's audio, but somehow messes up the written text. Arabic is read from right to left and almost all of the letters connect. For some odd reason, the developers decided to arrange the letters from left to right, which I'm assuming caused the letters to space out.

Anyone who has played a shooter knows how the developers try to humanize the main characters by using catchy nicknames and detailed background stories. Many shooters aim for realism, using current real-world conflicts or battlefields as an inspiration. Some video games are even developed with the help of ex- or current military personnel. When working on the latest entry in the popular *Medal of Honor*-series, for example, developer Electronic Arts hired real Navy Seals to act as paid consultants.

The problem is, the "authenticity" is only on one side. As an American, you get to relate to the hero defending his country from terrorists threatening your freedom. As an Arab, you get to relate to the guy who wants to blow up your city, and that's all. Often, it seems more time is spent making sure the guns in the game are authentic than on accurately representing the culture I belong to.

As a player, you are very rarely introduced to the enemy in a proper way. His appearance and overall character portrays only stereotypical substitutes for humanity; for example, in *Medal of Honor: Warfighter*, the brown and dusty gown, dark skin, thick beard, AK-47 in hand, and bare feet all come into play

Obviously, this isn't really what our lives are like. Over here we've got our stoners, jocks, rockers, preppies—just like anywhere else. But in the games we play, we don't see anything but stereotypes.

And of course, we never ever hear about an Arab's story in these games, nor their families or background. We never know why these "terrorists" are always attacking the red, white, and blue forces of justice. Usually, all we are told is that they are planning something radically dangerous and they need to be stopped. We are never even really given a real motive.

It's not hard to see why. If we did, that would humanize them, and that probably wouldn't be as fun. The less you can relate to guy at the other end of your rifle, the easier it is to shoot his head clean off.

These discrepancies—including the poor Arabic I mentioned earlier—add to the disconnect between me and my digital counterpart. Of course, I'm aware at the end of the day that this is all fiction. The stereotypes are there to support certain gameplay scenarios. But as more and more military-themed shooters come along, the more the false projections are reinforced, and they are used not to make a point, but simply for entertainment.

As Arabs, whether we live abroad or in our home countries, we are used to being portrayed negatively. We aren't the only ethnicity to suffer from silent racism, but we have to deal with being imagined as "terrorists." I think having to deal with accusations of being radical, violent freedom-haters is worse than many other racial associations. It is a stereotype that is reinforced in movies, books, games, news, and even in real life situations like airport security checkpoints.

I think what separates being vilified in a movie from being vilified in a video game is that in games, you're the one pulling the trigger. You are actively shooting at the bad guys, as opposed to being just a witness or spectator. Interactivity is what distinguishes games from other media—and it is exactly that which makes the stereotypes so much worse.

As an Arab playing a shooter game, you're in a country you've probably visited before, and you know it looks nothing like how it is being depicted. You're shooting down militants who look nothing like modern-day Arabs and who speak a language that is nowhere near what you know it should sound like. The experience creates what I think is best described as a sort of pseudo-culture.

How does this personally make me feel? Indifferent, which is unsettling. In theory, all the negative portrayals in the media have just numbed me out. The fact that I've grown so accustomed to the typical stereotypes like the beard and brown gown (whether in a movie, book, TV show, or video game) worries me.

The very first time I saw an Arab portrayed in *Counter Strike*, I remember thinking it was hilarious. My reaction wasn't anger or frustration. I found it funny. I remember laughing every time I heard the "terrorists" spit out their pseudo-language. When I see a stereotypical Arab portrayed in a game, I simply don't associate that image with any part of my culture. This could be a good thing, but how I reached this point—the point where I don't even react when my own culture is being vilified—is the scary part.

With all this said, there is one thing I can safely say many Arab gamers will not tolerate seeing misrepresented in the games they play, and that is religion.

A few years ago, a popular Youtube gaming channel in the Middle East pointed something out, something that caused a pretty big uproar within the community. In one of the maps in *Modern Warfare 2*, a game that was pretty old at the time, is a picture frame in one of the many rooms. This picture frame held an engraving that read "Allah is beautiful and He loves beauty," which normally would be fine. However, this painting was hung in a bathroom, over a toilet.

If this painting was hung in any other room, no one would have cared. However, the Muslim faith teaches that it is offensive to have holy teachings in a bathroom. So a video was made that garnered almost a million views in a matter of days. The video was meant to point out the offensive material to Infinity Ward and announce that the Arab gaming community would boycott the franchise if nothing was done about it.

Now, *Call of Duty* is perhaps the most popular series of all in the Middle East. There are several million gamers in the region who play games in the franchise on a daily basis. I don't know if it was the threat of a boycott that made Infinity Ward go back to a game that was four years old at the time—meaning that four other, newer installments had been released since the original—and patch the picture frame. But they did. The Favela map was removed from multiplayer rotation until Infinity Ward was able to remove the engraving.

The story of the picture frame is important, because it shows that it is possible to change things. For maybe the first time ever, the Arab gaming community came together and revolted over the picture frame. Infinity Ward listened and made changes.

What worries me is how seldom this happens. Countless other stereotypical and vilifying depictions of Arabs seem to go completely unnoticed. Why did the painting in the bathroom enrage thousands, while the constant, primitive and offensive depictions of our entire culture stir absolutely no emotions in most people?

I don't know the answer to that question, but I guess what I am trying to say is that we are well aware of how we are often perceived in video games. We notice. But given all the misconceptions about us in other media—newspapers, TV-series, and movies—I just don't think we care anymore.

In one way or another, I guess we've all grown a little numb.

Hussein Ibrahim is the former editor in chief of At7addak.com, *one of the largest Arab-language video game websites. He grew up in Detroit and is currently based in Beirut, Lebanon.*

A Game I Had to Make

ZOE QUINN

Game developer Zoe Quinn has described her game *Depression Quest* as "interactive (non)fiction about living with depression." The game is interactive fiction by form, but nonfiction in how it attempts to capture the daily experience of living with depression as honestly as possible. In this essay, Quinn reveals the story of how the game came to be, and why it's not meant to be fun.

IT'S 2:00 P.M. ON A SATURDAY, THE MIDDLE OF THE WORKDAY, and you're sitting on a curb coughing and crying so hard you're not sure which tears are from what. It's the first time in a long time you've cried—normally you're too low or too numb to even have the energy, but you've just found yourself with a window of opportunity thanks to losing your awful minimum-wage coffee shop job, having walked off after being denied a day off to try and get your pneumonia taken care of. This job was your only source of income. You don't know what you're going to do now.

You have one project half finished that you've barely touched since starting it with a partner who has left you hanging both as a collaborator and girlfriend. He bailed two weeks into the game and you can't really blame him, since he's wrestling with the enormity of his own depression, but you feel abandoned and the relationship is rapidly deteriorating around you. You're trying to be the strong one for him while fighting to keep your own head above water. You started out together on a mission to create a piece of media that would exist as an alternative to the false depictions of the illness you both live with. Since you see depression as a system with certain rules that you have to operate within and push against, translating that into a game mechanic made sense as a way to try to communicate your experience. It was a good idea, but your partner has been swallowed whole by the illness that was nipping at his heels, and you are alone now, having announced the game and thus staked your name on finishing it. You've been working on it after work when you can, when you aren't too exhausted, but the days only seem to get longer and your emotional condition worse.

Now, you feel completely lost. Even though you hated your job, it was your source of income. You sink your head in your hands, hyperventilate through wheezes, and panic, until your sense of shame at crying in public overtakes you and you make your way home. You look through job postings for all the local game studios, despite being asked at your last interview at a studio what you did to deserve sexual harassment in the industry. You come up empty-handed. You don't even want a studio job, but you have no savings or family support and would prefer it to being on the streets again, and it seems like a cushy position compared to cleaning bathrooms despite being able to program. You apply to a swath of manual labor and entry-level positions on Craigslist, and feel desperate. You know this is what you have to do every day for *who knows how long*, and that this part beats the part after, where you've applied to everything you can and are just alone with your thoughts—the same thoughts that lately have felt like your brain turning on itself in an act of autocannibalism.

Now what? you wonder.

You half wish that you'd stayed at your job and just let the pneumonia get worse because at least you'd know you have somewhere to live next month. You don't really know anyone in your neighborhood well enough to talk to, other than your similarly afflicted partner, and you're trying hard to keep it together for him.

You open Twine and look at your game about depression. You figure you might as well finish it, given that you have all the time in the world combined with the crushing weight of your illness on your back. But you need to promise yourself. You need a motivator to keep you from falling off the tightrope you feel like you have only one toe left on.

You set up a camera. You haven't announced a launch date for the game and now is as good a time as any—publicly posting it forces you to then do *something* about it, and maybe the game's impending release will motivate your partner to action too, even if that just means being supportive of you while you finish it. But when do you release it?

Valentine's Day is two weeks away. Is that too snarky? Do you really care if it is?

Most launch dates come with a trailer. How do you make a trailer for interactive fiction? You can't exactly mimic the industry standard of slapping dubstep on some slow-motion shots of your grizzled protagonist doing something summarily badass. Your game is full of words and focuses on wrestling with your mental states. How do you show that on camera?

You set up your webcam, deciding to try to communicate the

overall point of the game instead of doing some kind of features list. The game is all about how the illness removes choices and takes things away. You do what seems most honest while staying true to what you're actually feeling. You decide to take a risk and be vulnerable because that's what the work is all about.

The trailer becomes thirty seconds of you in bed, eyes still red from crying and coughing, staring at the wall. You super-impose the title of the game and the release date on the empty white walls of your room, promising to ship the game a mere two weeks from today. Apathetic from a day of high emotion, you emotionlessly post it online, hoping that you can fight your demons hard enough to finish the game in time. You accept the possibility that you'll lose and destroy your reputation, but you have no one to talk to and don't know what else to do.

You sit down and do the only thing you feel like you can. You code.

× × ×

It's 4:00 a.m. on launch day. You've barely slept this week, having written over 38,000 words, plenty of which will not be seen on a given playthrough. You've taught yourself enough After Effects to animate four images for every single image in the game. Each image has a level of distortion correlating to the player's current level of depression. You've figured out a way to digitally duct-tape three layered tracks of music to play simultaneously, two of them dynamically generated based on player action. All of this is done for a game you think maybe a total of five people will play, figuring that four will not understand it and one will maybe go, "Huh, okay."

You pass through it to give it a fifth or so edit and bug check.

Seeing it almost finished like this is weird. You can see it as a whole instead of a series of things it could be. What you've ended up making is a second-person interactive semifiction that shows the player a series of everyday events and gives them options of what they would like to do. The first option is always the healthy, "correct" option that people who haven't struggled with depression would choose. That one is crossed off in bold red in front of the player. The rest of the options are less ideal and based on what is more realistic for someone struggling with depression. More and more of them get crossed off based on how the player has played, and how well they've managed their depression so far. Eventually, they get an ending based on a lot of factors decided during play, but you've made very sure that none of them result in "Oh, hey, you're cured. Good job, you won!"

The game you've made isn't fun, but that was never the point. It doesn't have a 3D or even 2D you can interact with. Despite being able to program those kinds of games, you've pushed their formats aside in favor of focusing on words and internal mental processes. You've made every design choice to serve the ethos and point of the game—to show what depression is like for people who don't have it, and to reach out to other people suffering with it to try to let them know they're not alone.

You weren't able to include everything about depression, and you decided early on not to try to. You thought about trying to tackle the huge topic of therapy and medication, and how depression sufferers can spend years trying to find just the right dose of just the right pill from just the right therapist, but in order to tackle that subject at all, and to do it justice, you'd have to make an entirely separate game. Similarly, you decide to stay away from the topic of suicide because in spite of it being related to depression, your own experiences with it make it feel like too big a subject to tackle in a game that is only two hours long for a playthrough. You also worry about players playing the game to try and make the point-of-view character kill themselves, or otherwise using it as a tool to be sadistic. You're not trying to make emotional snuff.

Part of you also secretly worries that if you go down that route, you'll end up in a worse place yourself. Writing the game has been emotionally gut-wrenching. While your own relationship was crumbling around you, writing the parts where the love interest is supportive and understanding was even harder. You had to enforce a policy on yourself to actively stop writing if the encounters turned into a litany of you simply berating yourself.

Remembering this, you delete several nodes that are unlinked to any content, remnants of those entries. You try not to read several thousand words written to yourself, telling you how awful at life you are. You've already tried to strike a balance between being honest while drawing on personal experience and making the game about the illness, not you. To create distance, you have given the protagonist every advantage in life you wish you might have had—a job, a loving family, a supportive and understanding partner, pills that work, and a therapist who could be effective—while in reality you have none of these. It is more important to focus on the fact that depression can strike anyone regardless of their station in life, as well as to show how all of those advantages can be impacted by the illness. The game is meant to be a 101 introduction to the concept, not a definitive tell-all.

You have left the point of view character genderless. It was easier for you as a queer person to write from this perspective. The love interest started out genderless as well but morphed into a coherent person cobbled together from a cluster of past girlfriends of yours and your partner's—you take the plunge and make her a woman. Gender in games matters to you as someone so constantly alienated by how it is usually portrayed, so you try to do the right things in your own work.

The game seems as finished as it's going to be. You've uploaded the game, making it browser based and free. All you have to do is post a link. That's the only thing left.

You stare blankly at your monitor. Part of you is convinced that no one is going to play this or understand it even if they do. Half of you is fairly sure you're outing yourself as a nutter, exposing to the entire world all these parts of yourself that you hate and wish were gone, but you take a small comfort in knowing that likely no one will choose to play it. The other half of you stands behind your work and sincerely hopes that in doing something as terrifying as indiscriminately outing yourself as mentally ill and drowning in it, maybe you can help someone else. Dear god, you hope you can help someone else. You're similarly split over hoping that you're the only person who feels this way because feeling this way is terrible, and hoping you're not alone and can help a hypothetical someone else.

Either way, you're fairly sure most people will write you off as crazy.

You push the button to tweet out the link anyway.

× × ×

It's a little over a month after launch, and you're in San Francisco during the Game Developer Conference. It's the first time you've been around so many developers, and you are overwhelmed by how many of them know who you are. *Depression Quest* has been receiveing steady critical acclaim since its release and you've already reached ten thousand times the number of players you were expecting. There have been think pieces on it. Before this, you had no idea how many people were suffering from depression around you, likely because you were always too scared to out-and-out admit you were depressed, which seems to be a common thread in the conversations around the game that are ones of commisseration.

You are starting to meet people whose work you've looked up to since you started in game development a year and a half ago, and a lot of them have been touched by your work. You have always suspected that a lot of creative people have wrestled with depression, but since shipping the game, you've gotten a way better feel for exactly how many, and it's staggering. You're continously shocked by how many people tell you their stories in hushed tones, usually starting with the sentence: "I've never told anyone this but . . ." You desperately try to put your near-crippling social anxiety aside to listen to these intense and personal stories told to you by other depression sufferers. You know exactly how it feels to reach out about it only to be met with disappointment. Several academics and therapists tell you they're incorporating the game into their work, and it breaks your brain. You stop arguing with people who tell you your work matters to them when a friend points out that you're shitting on their opinion, and even if you don't agree with them about the quality of your work, you can at least respect their opinion. You don't know how to handle this many people knowing you exist, much less caring about your work.

You have inadvertently become a beacon for the cause of depression. A massive conversation has begun around the game, sometimes positive, sometimes negative. The chief criticisms are of the protagonist's situation and positive experiences with therapy and medication; you took a calculated risk in depicting them as such. Your heart aches when people who have situations more similar to your own than to your protagonist's say they didn't see themselves in the game. Regardless, you're happy that a lot of people feel like they can talk about this enormous, invisible thing they have always been unsure of in the public eye.

The emails are harder to deal with. You made the game and put it out into the world hoping you could let people know they are not alone and that someone else shares their feelings. What you weren't expecting was how much you would get back. You get upward of ten lengthy emails a day from strangers, telling you their stories in more detail than anyone would dare face-to-face. The stories are beautiful, they are heartbreaking, and you are frequently moved to tears when these people tell you that your game helps them. Several of them have adopted cats, gone back into therapy, or sought help because of the game. A few say you saved their lives, and those are the ones who instantly cause you to break down. They don't know that you almost successfully ended your own life and that the only reason you're alive and could make the game in the first place is because of the intervention and care of a single person, the best human being that you have ever met in your entire life and the reason you try so hard to pay it forward. You don't know how to deal with it.

You swear to devote time to answering every single email. This feels impossible because every time you try to thank someone, or try to tell them how much it means to you that you could do some real good with a video game, everything you say feels like a platitiude. It sounds cheap in comparison to how it all feels.

There is some bad too but it's minor. You get the normal batches of creeps online that send you grossly sexual messages or tell you to get back in the kitchen. This barely fazes you because you have been online for a long time and are unimpressed at the lack of originality. Sometimes you respond with pithy short messages mocking them, sometimes you genuinely engage them if it seems like they are simply ignorant and not mean, and other times you just send them pictures of cats hoping that it helps them get over their own damage. It's nothing you can't handle, and you are too overwhelmed by the good to care too much about it.

× × ×

It's eight months after the game has been released, and you are on top of a roof freezing your ass off and stuffing sequins into an *Angry Birds* piggy bank with a friend. The day has been a nightmare and you've resorted to absurdism as a coping mechanism.

A few days ago, you recieved an anonymous email from a fan telling you that they loved *Depression Quest* and had to give you a warning. An Internet forum dedicated to depressed virgins had found out about your existence and they were pissed. The email told you to look out for phone calls and other things in the coming days, since these people were looking for you and were out for blood. Ignoring their warning, you google around and find the subculture in question and their threads about you. You laugh as you see them unironically write things like "women can't have depression they can lay in the street with their hole open and any man will come along and solve their problems," because it's so cartoonishly awful you can't take it seriously. You screengrab some of the worst stuff to send to a friend over Instant Messenger and think no more of it.

. . . until they start calling your phone a few days later. On the first call, you can clearly tell,someone is jerking off on the other end, grunting and making gross wet noises. Shortly after you hang up, another stranger calls and yells as many rape threats through the phone as he can before you hang up. You remember the warning email and put your phone into airplane mode, then you make a post on your private Facebook telling people to con- tact you through email or IM for the next few days. You ask them not to speak of it publicly because doing so would only make things harder on you. The game is already in *Steam Greenlight*'s Top 100 and getting on the platform was imminent anyway. You worry that if you say anything publicly people will attribute all of your success to people harassing you when you already had it in the bag. You were content to leave it at this.

A few months back, you put *Depression Quest* on *Greenlight*, the gateway to the largest digital distribution platform in the world, hoping to get the game to a wider audience that might not otherwise see it, and maybe to reach some new people that could be helped by it. *Greenlight* requires that small independent games be voted on by their community, leaving curation in the hands of a community known to shout racial slurs over voice chat and to use the word "rape" as a shorthand for nearly everything. Shortly after posting the game, you started recieving dozens of sexually explicit messages, detailed plans of how they were going to come to your house and rape or murder you, and other things of that nature. Given that you've been online since you were a little girl, this was nothing new to you and merely made you tired.

Then you had a message sent to your house. A handwritten note was delivered to your mailbox, talking about what they wanted to do to your body against your will. There was something chillingly personal about seeing it handwritten out like that, and given that you had enough going on at the time, you pulled the game off *Greenlight* as soon as the company announced they were eventually going to find a better way to operate.

Months passed and *Greenlight* remained (and still remains at the time of this writing) unchanged. You showed the game at a few festivals in the meantime, winning awards right and left, and meeting people really affected by your work. This made you bold again. You decided that if the game reached one more person that could be helped by it, then you could deal with the hate. It was a net positive in your mind. So you put the game back up.

But this time, they found your personal information. You made it semipublic while living in Boston during the Boston Marathon bombing because you coordinated a blood drive and efforts to shelter people displaced by the bombs. You knew the risks when putting your information out there, but it still seemed like the right thing to do.

You had not figured this would be the outcome.

Earlier in the day, when checking Twitter, you saw yet another scandal over a woman in game development having the audacity to do something. In particular, there was a conversation in which someone said the controversy had nothing to do with her gender. You look at your phone, unable to use it because of the harassment and rape threats that would blow it up if you turned it on. You think back on how this kind of thing happens multiple times a month, how that's only the ones you hear about, and how every single time people do the same mental backflips to try and say every incident is isolated, with no perception of how often they seem to be saying that.

You get mad.

You post the screengrabs that you snatched up a few days ago, daring anyone to tell you again that sexism in games isn't real when you can't even use your phone. You rant. You stand up for the other woman while knowing this will only really make things worse for you because any time you speak up, people seek to knock you down and call you a shrill harpy feminist. All you're doing is saying things that have happened.

Then a press outlet picks it up. Then another. Then another. With every one, the harassment intensifies. With every article about harassment of women in games, people come out of the woodwork to harass you for saying you were harassed. They do it with a level of self-awareness beneath that of a toddler.

Finally, you leave to go blow off steam with a friend who has nothing to do with games. You get perspective on how small the video game industry really is and how nice it is to step outside of it. When life feels heavy, it can be really important to remind yourself of how big everything else is and how in the grand scheme of things nothing can really be THAT big of a deal.

You decide to cope with everything feeling too big and too serious the best way you know how: by being totally absurd.

You and your friend find an *Angry Birds* piggy bank and fill it with sequins because, let's face it, you're still a game designer and care about particle physics. You climb up to the roof of the theater where he works at two in the morning, throw the stuffed bird off the roof, and scream "FUCK VIDEO GAMES!" into the night as a sacrifice to the gods of gaming for better luck. It's ridiculous. It's asinine. It's cathartic.

× × ×

It's over a year after the release of the game, and you're at Game Developer Conference again, but this time you're on stage. Your hands are shaking as you scroll through the notes of your talk on all of this and what it means and how to deal with it. You hope you don't sound as nervous as you are.

Your talk is a call to action.

Your conclusion is that Internet harassment is not something we can simply avoid or ignore. When digital distribution is the primary market of indie game developers, the Internet has become part of your workplace. Beyond that, the Internet is where so many of us find each other—where we build community—and for some developers who can't travel, it's the only community they'll ever have. Simply ignoring the problem in the hopes that it will go away doesn't do the value of these things justice.

When it started happening to you, you wanted to find out *why* people act like this online, and more importantly, how they might eventually stop or grow out of it. So you started talking to people. You put out a call saying, "Hey, if you used to do these things and stopped, please talk to me. No judgment, no call-outs, just casual conversation." And since then, you've talked to about three hundred people who have shared their stories with you. You've seen the following things over and over.

The number one thing they all had in common was that to some degree they didn't think of the person on the receiving end of their comments as a person. They depersonalized them as an abstract concept.

When asked about the ways that changed, almost all of them said that they "got better friends who wouldn't reinforce or tolerate their behavior" or "heard about it enough to realize it was a problem." Others said they ran into some small thing that humanized their targets.

None of these things were a specific turning point. Change moved at a glacier's pace and was cumulative, but this does give us some tools to figure out how to effect change now.

This means that "don't feed the trolls" has become largely useless advice. Calling this behavior "trolling" isn't being completely honest; it's harassment, pure and simple. You call on people to start calling it what it is. Suggesting that people stay silent in the face of harrassment only makes it harder for others to understand how these things impact people, and it doesn't move the needle that much closer to changing minds and behavior. It also isolates the people going through these things and makes them feel that speaking out or venting is somehow the wrong thing to do.

This also means that as hard and exhausting as it is to keep talking about and hearing these things because sometimes it feels like it's not actually helping, in reality you're putting drops in a bucket that will lead to things getting better. It's important to remember that every time you get stressed out by telling someone, "Hey, that's not cool," when they're being awful to someone else, you're really pushing progress forward even if you can't see it in the moment.

You know it's likely that not everyone can change or grow out of this behavior, but it's still a good assumption to start with since you can't tell who will or won't.

You say that taking care of ourselves and each other is important too. You tell the audience what helped you in the hopes that if they ever find themselves in a similar position, and you hope they don't, then this will maybe help them.

You tell them about the *Angry Birds* piggy bank and throwing it off the roof. You tell them it was completely asinine but it felt good to break from the feeling that everything was heavy and serious and stressful, and to just be goofy for a minute.

You say it also really helps to talk to people who have nothing to do with games at all, to mentally take a break from our microcosm. It helps to realize how small our world really can be in the grand scheme of things sometimes, and to remember there's a life outside video games.

Another thing you say is to save the worst of the harrassment and do dramatic readings in goofy voices with close friends. This especially helps if you do it with other developers who can do the same with their own awful comments. You feel that humor is an amazing way to heal yourself and others.

Additionally, when you're having one of those days where the Internet can feel like a place full of raging jerks, it helps to go do something nice for someone else. Doing this provides immediate proof that our microcosm's not all bad because you're going out there and actively making it better, and it's a reminder that in spite of how bad things can be sometimes, there's also a ton of good being done in and by online communities.

You encourage people not to feel bad about these things affecting them, either. "Should" can be the worst word in the English language—if someone feels like they SHOULDN'T care because it's "just the Internet," or because they know that these nasty comments aren't something to take seriously, it doesn't really mean much if they still DO feel that way. And that's fine—everyone's feelings are totally valid. Asking people to toughen up and "grow a thicker skin" doesn't usually result in anything other than having one more thing to feel like you're not doing right. There's no "right" way to feel, there's only how you're actually feeling. And it's important that people let themselves have that.

You hear a lot of developers who are privileged in one way or another tell you they don't feel like they can even be upset about the harassment they get when they compare it to what others from less privileged backgrounds receive. You ask them not to invalidate their own feelings just because they are socially conscious of their privilege. A straight white man will have a very different hate mail bag, but that doesn't mean it's empty or irrelevant. Instead, you ask people to try and use that feeling to build empathy for those who are worse off, not to disengage entirely.

You try to encourage everyone to talk about harrassment in any way they feel comfortable. If that's "not at all," that's fine as well. You encourage people to try and look out for themselves and to make sure they're okay first and foremost. Not everyone can try and fight back—even those who can can't do it every day—and that's not something to feel bad about either. You know it's asking a lot, but you ask people to be open if they can, to show how it's impacting them, to not retreat into a show-no-weakness PR voice. You acknowledge that it feels like opening yourself up for more hate, but being impacted and having feelings isn't a weakness, it's a simple reality. And hearing about that can not only change someone's mind and make them realize the consequences of their hatred—your voice can also end up being a positive force for other developers who might be feeling the same thing. They'll now know they're not alone, that someone else understands, and maybe they'll even find something in your story they can use in their own life to get through hard times. Someone might even reach out in response, give advice, stand up, or even just commiserate.

To you, that's really where the indie community shines. We excel at building communities, and the Internet community is one that needs some help to be better, safer, and less hostile. You tell the crowd that everyone has a game in them and a story only they can tell, and that for all the bullshit that happened to you, you don't regret making *Depression Quest*. Nothing can take away helping the people you helped. You claim that games are a powerful medium that can do a lot of good for a lot of people and tell stories and demand empathy through interaction in ways that other art forms don't, and as such, games matter. Nothing can make it not worth it, especially not Internet commenters with axes to grind.

You close by asking that instead of not feeding the trolls, we feed ourselves and each other.

Zoe Quinn is the developer of the critically acclaimed and award-winning game Depression Quest.

Your Humanity is in Another Castle: Terror Dreams and the Harassment of Women

ANITA SARKEESIAN and KATHERINE CROSS

Online harassment of pretty much anyone who does not present themselves as a straight white male is a persistent blight on tech and video game culture, and it emerged stronger than ever in the wake of the Gamergate controversy (see Dan Golding, page 127). In the following pages, Anita Sarkeesian and Katherine Cross take on the dynamics of online hate mobs in geekdom. They provide a scathing analysis of the murky sexism present in the video game world, recounting their own experiences with misogynist abuse.

Katherine's Story: The Priestess and the Wannabe Knight

It is a truth universally acknowledged that a Night Elf woman on her own in a digital world must be in want of a cyber husband.

Or so some would believe, at any rate.

This isn't the start of a piece of dreadful fan fiction, though I did have the misfortune of meeting someone who wanted to make it such. You see, for many years that lonely Night Elf was my character in the massively multiplayer online game (MMO) *World of Warcraft*. In that capacity I indirectly became the object of men's curiously expressed desires. While I was never a big deal in any reckoning of MMO hierarchy, I was certainly apt to meet hordes of people from atop my perch in front of Stormwind's bank, where my character often sold enchantments—a popular profession in the game, whereby one adds statistical value to the weapons and armor of other players.

It was here that I met many male gamers who often exceeded the bounds of good taste, and traipsed over the admittedly porous line between role-playing (RPing, or acting out the life of your avatar) and out-of-character behavior (simply acting as you yourself normally would). One fellow, who role-played as a Shaman, became smitten with me but couched his flirtations in the character of his avatar. I played along, always enjoying the RP I could pick up during server primetime.

Then our Shaman friend made his affections plain to me in chat that was clearly not role-play. I politely declined and suggested we just keep things fun and simple in clearly delineated RP. The plea fell on deaf ears. He plied me with gifts of gold and crafting materials, as well as routine offers of assistance in multiplayer dungeons, which sounds nice at first blush, but not when one considers the profoundly awkward balance sheet that seemed to linger in the background like a specter, on which I was indebting myself to someone who expected a rather metaphysical form of sugar in payment. Each time I was offered something, it created a stressful situation in which I had to refuse while also massaging his hurt feelings or his sense that I was ignoring him.

Worse was the ever-present fear of angering the man in question, which did happen on more than one occasion.

Truth be told, it's misleading to call what he was giving gifts. They were inducements, buttons being pressed on the vending machine of my womanhood in hopes that romantic affection would follow.

It was impossible to shift things back onto a level plane of friendship and in-game camaraderie, and it was only after he switched servers that I could exhale with relief. But the Shaman was hardly the last person to do this. I was stalked in-game by another male player who had taken my friendliness as a sign that he should pursue me amorously IRL, confessing to me in lengthy chat conversations that he fantasized about me lying on his open-shirted chest while he serenaded me with a guitar. I hardly knew the fellow. I just knew him as a Mage I sometimes quested and chatted about in-game politics with.

I'll never forget the day he stripped off his avatar's clothes and made it pose naked beneath a lava waterfall while he flirted with me. That was the last straw before I had to finally block him.

× × ×

Fast-forward to 2014, and I'm delivering a paper to other students in my graduate fellowship program. It is about online harassment, its causes, and how some game designers are trying to end it. One earnest young man raises his hand and compliments my presentation before launching into a lengthy disquisition of a question. He laments the fact that, in his mind, women in games like *World of Warcraft* are always being offered gifts and assistance because they are "girls," and maybe women should be forthright about refusing such "gifts" and stop giving men "the wrong idea." Women are "part of the problem," he says.

If only he could've walked a mile in my shoes on the streets of Stormwind.

Anita's Story: The Feminist and the Angry Mob

In the spring of 2012, I launched a fundraising campaign on the crowdfunding website Kickstarter, to create a series of videos that would examine the way women are represented in games. The project was called *Tropes vs. Women in Video Games*, and I asked for six thousand dollars to help make five long-form critical video essays on the subject.

I was enormously skeptical that I would be able to make my initial fundraising goal within the thirty-day window, but much to my surprise the project was fully funded within twenty-four hours and even far surpassed my financial goal as the weeks went by. I was absolutely elated that so many people were interested in a critical feminist analysis of games. As more backers contributed to the project, I introduced stretch goals to increase the number of videos I would produce as well as to expand the scope and range of the research area.

About two weeks went by and it occurred to me that I should let my YouTube channel subscribers know what I was up to. I uploaded my fundraising video, sent out a notification, and went to sleep. In the very early hours of the next morning, I received a call from a friend, urgently telling me to wake up to look at my YouTube video: it was flooded with hundreds upon hundreds of violently misogynist and racist threatening comments.

I didn't realize it at the time, but this was just the beginning of something that would fundamentally change my professional and personal life.

Over the next few days, all my social media sites were flooded with threats of rape, violence, sexual assault, and death.

The Wikipedia article about me was vandalized with sexism, racism, and pornographic images.

Campaigns were started to report all of my social media accounts, including my Kickstarter, my YouTube channel, and my Twitter account, as fraud, spam, and even terrorism in an effort to get them suspended and taken down.

Harassers attempted to knock my website offline, and to hack into my email and other accounts.

They attempted to collect and distribute my personal information, including my home address and phone number, as well as that of my family members.

Mini campaigns were organized to report me to the FBI and IRS. Harassers concocted outlandish conspiracy theories, including one that insisted my legitimate fundraising efforts were actually an act of fraud.

Pornographic images were drawn and fabricated of my likeness being raped by video game characters. These images were posted publicly on various websites and sent to me repeatedly, often disguised as fanmail.

One especially motivated harasser made a small flash game where players were invited to "beat the bitch up." Upon clicking on the screen, a photographic image of me would become increasingly battered and bruised.

Dozens of fake social media accounts were set up to impersonate me. These accounts then posted false quotes attributed to me that were designed to paint me as an unhinged extreme feminist. Those false quotes were copied, reposted, and shared across the Internet as a way to try and discredit me and my project.

Hours upon hours of angry, hateful, and conspiracy-laden video responses were made to spread disinformation, false rumors and straight-up lies.

Lengthy digital documents were created and published that included every piece of information harassers could find about me, including former employment, education, test scores, various addresses and contact information, previous hobbies and interests, personal photographs and videos. They didn't stop with me, however, and went on to collect further data about my team members, my friends, and my family.

Imagine an exploding geyser: a never-ending, violent, and steady eruption of toxic misogynist hate.

If there was a virtual venue for their hatred available, the harassers used it. Geysers of abuse streamed from every possible source, their torrents flooding into the physical realities of my everyday life.

This steady stream of misogynist harassment was startling in its variety. Some messages shared detailed examples of sexual acts harassers would like to commit against my body. Some showed images of ejaculation on a printed photograph of my face, others implicitly encouraged violence by publicly sharing and distributing my home address, or explicitly so, by sending death threats directly to me and bomb threats to organizers of events I speak at. This misogynist harassment still informs almost every aspect of my life. It informs what I can and cannot say. It informs where I can and cannot go. It keeps me and my loved ones on edge and in a constant state of fear.

When living under such a public and targeted microscope, the most mundane activities are treated as potential security threats. What was once simple and thoughtless—playing games online—is now a source of isolation and fear. Whether playing for pleasure or work, I guard my gamertags like precious metals; I don't play online multiplayer games with friends, and in the rare instances that I do go online, I permanently mute my mic and turn off my camera. Even with all that, I still regularly fear that my settings might somehow be reset without my notice.

All this because I offered a critical opinion of gaming—a hobby I've been engaged with all my life and care deeply about.

× × ×

Our two stories seem rather different—aggressive, pitched, and vicious harassment versus seemingly less intrusive creepery that even involved gift giving. What connects them? Are they even the same thing? Broadly speaking, yes they are. Each of our stories tells a different tale of sexual harassment: the gendered experience of being targeted against our will simply for being women online.

What connects our stories is the fact that some men in the world of gaming feel a sense of entitlement to control the presence of women online. Either we are their romantic sidekicks, or we must be silent. For Anita, a critic of video game culture, there is an implicit demand that she be silent and go away; for Katherine, her would-be paramours want to play the knight to her damsel (not coincidentally a popular trope in gaming that Anita has critiqued). In both cases, we were supposed to have no say in the outcome.

x x x

Online gaming culture hosts a bewildering variety of harassment—Anita was attacked by cybermobs, while Katherine was targeted by individuals acting alone—but each incident grows out of the same wider culture that promotes an unhealthy relationship between men and women, casting men as valiant defenders of cyberspace and women as henpecking invaders who will take away the boys' toys. The same thing was at work when former BioWare writer Jennifer Hepler was viciously harassed by thousands of online attacks that even penetrated into her home life in the form of threatening voicemails, and threats to her children. It was at work when *Gamespot* editor Carolyn Petit was attacked by cybermobs who loathed her for giving *Grand Theft Auto V* a 9/10 score, partly because of what she regarded as its sexist characterization of women, and this incident included a number of especially vicious attacks against her for being transgender.

But these are the big, attention-getting stories that involve such huge mobs they can't help but garner media attention. They're the tip of an iceberg that involves far more quotidian harassment directed at countless women whose names you've never heard of. In every case, for many of the harassers, it's just a game to them.

In many of these situations, gamers have concocted a grand fiction in which they are the heroic players of a massively multiplayer online game, and must work—alone or in concert—to take down the target and regain control. Or perhaps to romance the target. In this game, the targets are women. We imagine that to many readers it must seem flippantly appalling to think of such abusive acts as a game of some sort, but it is worth taking a moment to further examine this analogy to help us better understand how these things happen.

Since we need people to play a game, let's start with who the players are. The harassers are overwhelmingly male. According to the Entertainment Software Association, the average age of gamers in the United States is thirty years old. So while it may be our knee-jerk reaction to exclusively accuse teenage boys of such brazen behavior, it is both boys and men participating in this so-called game, and often they do so in groups of hundreds or even thousands at a time.

Where is this game played? Perpetrators turn the entire Internet into a battlefield. Online gaming environments, from pre- and post-game lobbies to in-game chat, are all fair locations for everything from unwanted sexual advances to rape and death threats. Social media, personal websites, and comments on articles are all popular spots for endless varieties of harassment. In addition to the battlefield (especially in larger cybermob attacks), perpetrators keep a home base where they communicate with one another, coordinate their raids, and generally work together. This usually takes place on largely unmoderated and largely anonymous message boards and forums with no real mechanisms for accountability.

Now, we don't usually think of online harassment as a communal activity, but we know from the strategies and tactics most commonly used that many players are actually loosely coordinating with one another. This interactive aspect leads us to pinpoint this game's genre: a massively multiplayer online game.

"Playing" in a social group is a powerful motivating factor that provides incentives for perpetrators to participate and to escalate the onslaught to earn the praise and approval of their peers. We can kind of think of this as an informal reward system where players earn "Internet points" for increasingly brazen and abusive activities. In many cases, harassers document their attacks via screenshots and bring them back to home base as evidence to show off to each other—like trophies or achievements.

Every game needs some kind of goal or endgame. In this one, women are kind of like the ball being tossed between competing men. Other times we're the point system. Still other times, we're the damsel waiting to be rescued and victoriously smooched by the gentleman hero. More often than not, we're the final boss in need of a strategic takedown, barring the way between the male player and his final triumph. In every case, we are an object—a non-player character (NPC), if you like—but never the stars of our own stories, never players in our own right. One way or another, we are passive digital matter in men's stories. If you want to know what "objectification" means, that's a good place to start.

Our game metaphor grows out of Anita's study of her own harassment and Katherine's sociological work on the wider phenomenon of harassment in gaming. Both of our analyses converge on one key point: harassment happens because the dehumanization it entails takes the shape of gaming itself, with all the suggestions of play and inconsequentiality therein. If it's just a game, then it's not real, and if it's not real then no one can get hurt and no harm is truly done. The corollary to this, of course, is that if people believe no one is really being hurt, then no one will be punished or held accountable for the harm.

Perverted Passions

But an astute reader might well ask: if it's not real to the harassers, then why do they care so much? Why do they want to stop Anita from doing her work? Why did those guys in *WoW* want to be Katherine's boyfriends? The answer lies in the fact that our behavior in gaming spaces can never be fully divorced from reality. Transfeminist writer Autumn Nicole Bradley put it best when she said in an interview, "Players don't get 'fake time' and 'fake emotional reserves' to play in a 'fake world.' It's still players' real time and real emotional investment in their characters and their actions."

This is part of the reason why gaming is so important to us as committed gamers. It's why we spend hours grinding for achievements, debating technical or narrative minutiae, bashing our heads against the walls of tough bosses or raids, and just generally being fans of the games we love. It takes energy, and it engenders a kind of commitment, even if you intellectually know that "it's just a game."

Yet gaming culture also induces us to adopt its basic conceit of "play." All gaming takes place within what has long been famously called "the magic circle" of play—a special realm exempt from the rigors and responsibilities of "the real world." When your character dies in a video game, after all, no one is actually hurt. It's all experimental theater in the name of good fun.

But when you add socializing into the mix through online multiplayers, say, such as one finds in *Guild Wars 2, League of Legends,* or *Call of Duty*, it puts human interaction between *real people* in the magic circle. The conceit that "this isn't real" bleeds into our online interactions, even as we commit ourselves deeply to the space as fans and players.

In this way, the gaming world is—from the perspective of the average player—both real and unreal at the same time.

This is what Katherine calls "the mobius strip of reality and unreality." A mobius strip is a rather fun mathematical object that has only one side and one boundary, but gives the illusion of having two sides. It collapses both sides into a single, unbounded surface. It's a useful way of thinking about how our view of reality works in gaming. It explains why some people can be so threatened by the work of feminist gamers while feeling free to subject them to vicious harassment because they sincerely believe it's "just words," "not real," or "just a game."

For too many male gamers, the world of gaming is something they perceive as a boy's clubhouse: a refuge from the stresses of the "real world." This gives them a very real emotional stake in policing its integrity. One man who complained bitterly about Anita's project began his rant by saying: "Video games are the last bastion of male entertainment that hasn't been constantly under attack, threatened, or attempted to be neutered." The conceit of play means that a wider panoply of options are open to gamers when they want to defend that "last bastion" from outsiders, including things they would never consider saying or doing, say, to a co-worker or a relative, at least not in person.

The Internet acts as a kind of dissociative interface that makes it easy to forget you're dealing with human beings. It's not a question of anonymity, necessarily. Just check your Facebook. People saying awful things to one another is hardly limited by having their real names and faces attached to it; the idea that people will eschew prejudice once they are forced to "put their names to it" is mostly false.

Anonymity online plays its role in giving people another way of shirking accountability, but the broader problem is that even if you aren't wearing a mask, this behavior is so commonplace and acceptable that few will even bother trying to hold you accountable for cyberbullying or harassment.

This isn't about anonymity; it's about dehumanization.

Combine that with sexism in "the real world," still persisting in ways great and small, a popular culture that still conceives of women as technological dupes and wet blankets who ruin the fun, and the deep emotional investment that all gamers have in their games and communities, as well as how that bleeds over into web forums, Twitter, and even "real world" conventions . . . and you have a recipe for, well:

> *"All feminists must die, if I found out where you live, I will rapo u to death!"*

> *"I think you just need to let out that frustration you just need a good dicking, I'll fuck you in the bumhole if you want"*

> *"I will fucking come to your house tonight and rape you dry (srs) prepare your anus"*

> *"I would lick all of your body.. And then cum on your whore mouth. Just to let you know who has the real POWER."*

"I want to hate fuck your face."

"maybe if anita sarkeesian gets raped in the throat hole hard enough she'll stop making words"

"I hope you get raped you stupid cunt."

"Oh wow, typical fucking stupid CUNT TWAT SLUT WORTHLESS CUM RECEPTACLE. Go ahead and don't approve my comment, this one is just for you. Enjoy getting raped honey, I'm coming for you."

"U know who's REALLY creepy? Man hating shit like you. Pls get breast cancer,die in writhing agony While getting raped"

"Calm down, Anita. You can just ignore this and no harm done. They won't actually rape you throug the Internet."

"I ask God every night to kill you with brain cancer. Let's all hope he comes through so we don't see Lara Croft in a winter parka"

"Kill yourself you dumb cunt"

"How much would you pay for a video of Feminist Frequency's writer being raped by a group of angry black men?"

"I find your videos easy to masturbate to . . . with the mute option on of course. #masturbatingonfeminism"

"You don't play games and don't know anything about games."

"Anita is not a gamer. REAL gamers don't nick pick things that don't matter to the overall enjoyment of the game."

"The game isn't for girls anyway. Get back to the kitchen if you don't like it."

"FUCK YOU, I'M GONNA KICK YOU IN THE PUSSY."

"I hate ovaries with a brain big enough to post videos."

"That isn't misogyny. It's just that computers, and video games as well, were never meant for women."

"Women don't belong in video games."

These are some of the comments Anita received.

Our passions are real. They are part of what make gaming a fun refuge for us all, in different ways. But societal sexism can pervert those passions, turning them into fuel for all that harassment. There is a particular kind of gamer passion that inherently excludes outspoken women whose ideas are deemed an existential threat to the boys' club. Even though the club was always something of a fiction—women have been a part of the gaming world as players, designers, writers, coders, and fans from the start—it is a fantasy these men cannot distinguish from reality. The abiding belief that their sacred refuge is under attack inspires the sheer terror evident in these comments.

What about the argument that these hateful, bigoted, rude,

and crude remarks are "just words"? The old adage "sticks and stones may break my bones, but names will never hurt me" rings false here, as it does in the rest of the world. That notion has always misunderstood what language is for: naming and shaping reality. These misogynist words and actions actually do hurt, and they also do much more than that. The women who are targeted by harassers, whether it be a handful of comments or years of constant hate, are not left unscathed by the experience. We are often told to "grow a thicker skin" or to "just ignore it," but these dismissive statements are ultimately asking women to put up with the daily abuse. It is asking us to jettison our own humanity in order to participate in a pastime, fandom, or professional environment that we all hold dear.

Dismissing such attacks as "just the way the Internet is" or as "playful trolling" denies the emotional consequences and trauma that women experience when faced with such abuse. It ignores the very real silencing of women who are forced to remove themselves from online communication, engagement, and play in order to shield themselves from further assault. In reality, this means women lose all the benefits of digital connectedness, from friendships to professional associations. But it isn't only the immediate victims who suffer. It's those who silently bear witness as well. Women who are bystanders to harassment and abuse are discouraged from speaking up or participating in gaming spaces for fear of being the next target.

In short, the end result is that these harassment tactics work to reinforce and normalize a culture of sexism and misogyny—wherein men who harass are supported and rewarded by their peers, and women are silenced, marginalized, and excluded.

The Terror Dream

This harassment finds its ultimate fuel in latent misogyny and other prejudices. Evidence abounds to suggest that women are yet to achieve equality in most sectors of our society, and so it shouldn't surprise us that the subculture of gaming is no different in this regard. But there are other social factors at work. Earlier, we talked a bit about how the passion of gaming fandom is often turned to perverse ends, and this dovetails with one of the other major challenges facing gamer culture: a deep aversion to change.

For many hardcore gamers, particularly men who span the multigenerational legacy of gaming culture, there is a profound terror of what lurks around the corner of the next E3, the next AAA release, or the next developer announcement. You see it, for instance, among older MMO players who have a great deal of nostalgia for the earliest MMOs like *Everquest*, lauding their notoriously unforgiving and tedious systems as true challenges befitting *real* gamers. You see it in the hyperbolic anger that greeted *Mass Effect 3*'s controversially minimalist ending, where online rants imbued the ending with dramatically outsized importance, heralding the death of role-playing games, advanced storytelling, and perhaps life as we know it. You also see it in the still-smoldering rage that attended *Dragon Age 2* because of its perceived deficiencies; it too was seen by some as a harbinger of the gamer apocalypse.

In each case, there is a terror dream lurking beneath the surface. It is a fear that someone, somewhere is going to take gaming away from the nerdy fans who've huddled around its warmth as a refuge from the world's bullying. The culture wars of the '80s and '90s provided fuel for this fear—from religious extremists lambasting *Dungeons & Dragons* as a Satanic tool, to the headline-grabbing moral crusades of former Senator Joe Lieberman, or lawyer Jack Thompson who sought outright bans on video games, to the tragically successful efforts of the Australian government at doing so. These events left a cultural scar on gamers of all backgrounds. But gamers also fear corrosion from within: every merger, every new release, every hiring and firing wave, and every attempt to do something new is greeted with morbid suspicion. Could this be the day gaming is destroyed forever?

It is this violent mix of rational and irrational fears that misogyny enters into. Women—even women gamers and game developers—are placed in the category of "threats." Women are perceived as one of the great existential assaults on the world of gaming that could take it all away forever. Feminist gamers and critics, for instance, are routinely lumped in with right-wing extremists, as if we seek destructive or censorious bans on gaming rather than cultural acceptance of the women who are already here.

This attitude doesn't spare women leaders in the video game industry itself. Earlier, we mentioned the case of Jennifer Hepler, who ended up fighting waves of virulent online harassment. But why? Because enterprising 4channers and Redditors dug up what was, by then, a six-year-old interview with Hepler in which she opined that she would like to see role-playing games where one could skip unwanted combat as easily as one could skip dialogue. For this suggestion alone she was pilloried as a woman who "hated gaming," wanted to "destroy gaming," and whose contributions to gaming were irredeemably feminine and "gay."

All this happened in spite of Hepler being a writer for BioWare, whose most successful titles are beloved among gamers. She wrote for some of its most acclaimed franchises, but this did not render her immune to this genre of hateful criticism. She was deemed a "bitch" who was irreversibly an outsider. Worse, she was imagined as a pathogen to the body of gaming itself. This is also why Carolyn Petit took all the flak that she did. For lightly lacerating one of the sacred cows of gamer culture (and one of its most static franchises, at that), Petit was met with a flood of transmisogynist hatred.

This fear metastasizes into racism very easily as well. One sees this in the racism and anti-Semitism that laced many attacks on Anita, as well as in cultural memes like the stereotype of the "Chinese gold farmer" in multiplayer RPGs. Laboring under exploitative conditions in Asian and Eastern European countries, gold farmers rapidly acquire in-game currency that is then sold to mostly Western gamers for real-world money. Even as gamers line up to buy the gold, they condemn the "farmers," and in turn any player they deem to be Asian, who is automatically presumed both a cheat and a worthy target of mockery and harassment. A common complaint is that Asian gamers are wrecking in-game economies. What emerges is a vision of rapacious people of color corrupting a game that is perceived not only as a male pastime, but a largely white one at that.

This is the nexus of misogyny, racism, and fear of change. The terror dream that male gamers in particular keep reliving is one in which imaginary mega moms try to take their toys away from them, whether in the guise of church, state, corporation, or an actual flesh-and-blood woman.

There is no doubt that gaming is currently in a state of flux, particularly as gaming is swallowed whole by big money and corporate blandness. Many of the changes are less than healthy. But, ironically, many of these corporations trade on the gamers' fear of change. There is a reason that all those successive *Calls of Duty* and *Medals of Honor* all look the same, save some graphic updates here and there.

The anger that this knee-jerk fear and weird conservatism generate flows right into latent misogyny. The resulting psychic explosion is what makes up the violent geysers of hatred experienced by Anita and all too many others.

But there's another piece to the puzzle, and it's where Katherine's erstwhile Lotharios reenter the picture.

The Entitlement Complex

The link between Katherine's experience with mild sexual harassment in *WoW* and Anita's with overt deluges of outright hatred is the issue of entitlement. For too many men in the world of gaming, if the presence of women is to be suffered, we must exist as another prop in the world for their pleasure. It is no small part of why so much art in games portrays borderline pornographic images of women contorted and proportioned for maximum stereotypical viewing pleasure. This differs from the bulky space-marine idealization of male characters because the latter are designed to be fantasies of action and power for the (presumably male) player. The sexualized women are mainly there to be looked at, consumed. It shouldn't surprise us if real women gamers are in turn looked at in much the same way.

If a game is to have a woman character, then she must be young and pretty. If a game is to have a woman player, then she must be two things: silent and sexually available.

This is entitlement's dark heart: the belief that these gamers are owed the full range of a woman's agency and personhood. To be a woman who speaks on voice chat in a multiplayer game, for instance, entails a risk that men almost never have to consider. If you aren't suddenly inundated with tired sandwich "jokes," you'll be asked to somehow show your tits, or you'll otherwise be flirted with—even if you say no.

To "out" yourself as a woman in a multiplayer game is often a very difficult and fraught decision because you'll immediately be treated differently. But it can happen even if you don't outright confirm that you're a woman. Katherine, for example, never told the male gamers who flirted with her that she was a woman; they just assumed she was and behaved as if she was. She wasn't opposed to gaming with them or to role-playing with them—that's why she was there, after all—but she had a right to say she wasn't there to pick up a real-life partner.

The fact that her clear statements of "no" were refused is itself a sign of the problem. She first begged off their advances, then explicitly said she was not interested. It didn't matter. They didn't listen and kept at it until major interventions prevailed upon the men to stop. One changed servers, the other was blocked. Their inability to hear Katherine, however, was part and parcel of the very issue of entitlement that also causes more extreme forms of harassment.

Conclusion: Are Women Gamers Human?

Our stories aren't all bad. Katherine remembers her time in *WoW* fondly and still plays MMOs whenever she can; Anita grew up with video games and is still jubilant whenever a new *Kirby* game is released. We are not only victims, and no one deserves to be defined as such. That's one of the quiet tragedies of harassment—it collapses the diversity and contradiction of human experience into moments of trauma.

To even talk about it runs the risk of validating the mentality of the harasser: that the targets are somehow less than human, defined only by how their attacker sees them. But for those of us who speak out, we do not treat either ourselves or the people we advocate for simply as victims. We recognize what their attackers did not: they are human, fellow gamers, and part of our nerdy little community, with their own stories to tell, and their own personhood and distinctiveness to add to the mosaic of gaming.

And that is where we as gamers can begin to make meaningful change. For male gamers tempted to excuse or minimize this harassment, or who claim gaming as a space "for guys," we ask them to start seeing women in the community as being gamers like themselves—rather than outsiders or invaders, even (or perhaps especially) when we are being critical—and to remember that everyone they interact with online is a real person, not just another pixellated enemy to be slain.

We would say, "We come in peace," if that didn't imply we weren't already here. Both of us have had keyboards and controllers in our hands since we were kids; women were playing games since before there was a Ms. Pac-Man. Women have been on the development teams of countless beloved titles. We didn't just come in peace, we've helped make gaming what it is.

In this chapter, we've tried to show how a sexist vision of women as perpetual strangers to gaming and technology has combined with other cultural issues within the world of gaming to produce a profoundly hostile environment. The forces we've discussed also shape the dynamics of racism, homophobia, and transphobia in gaming, with each target group similarly being seen and targeted as hyperpolitical outsiders.

At its best, gaming can be a wonderful escape, but it is also very much a demon-haunted virtual world, burdened with the weight of its history and the travails of societal prejudices that we import into our play. To wit: so many male gamers live in fear of having their games taken away, banned, or destroyed from within. But it's time to wake up from the terror dream: the games aren't going anywhere. Neither are women, for that matter.

The criticisms brought by feminists can be part of a wide ranging, thoughtful discussion in which people are free to agree and disagree, as dictated by their consciences. But what has happened so far is not conversation; it is abuse, plain and simple, motivated by prejudice against women. If our gaming worlds are going to change for the better, then we shall have to walk the well-worn paths of every other art form and recognize that not all criticism is an existential threat.

We have to remember that even as we play in our beloved online worlds, we are always dealing with other human beings. We have to relearn our sense of ethics for the online world and see an avatar as being a person not unlike ourselves. If gaming can change the world, it will do so as a sort of moral playground for relearning how to be human in a virtual universe.

By seeing your fellow female players as people (call it the radical idea of cyber-feminism), then we'll be one giant step closer to that beautiful future.

Anita Sarkeesian is a media critic and creator of the groundbreaking Feminist Frequency *video series. Katherine Cross is a sociologist and PhD student specializing in online harassment and gender in virtual worlds.*

The End of Gamers

DAN GOLDING

In fall 2014, the ever-present harassment of women in tech and gaming culture took a new and unprecedented turn with the Gamergate controversy. In reaction to a wave of new and progressive game criticism, the online hordes of so-called Gamergate made it their mission to silence their detractors. They claimed the identity of the gamer was being bullied by corrupt journalists in conspiracy with feminist critics. They were under threat, and this movement named for its Twitter hashtag #gamergate was a way to strike back. The strikes, however, had all the hallmarks of a reactionary movement—the Tea Party of the gaming world—and seemed more interested in harassment than anything else. In his take on Gamergate, Dan Golding presents a gamer identity that does not deny being threatened, but instead confirms and welcomes its imminent death as part of a narrow-minded, male-dominated subculture that has run its course.

WHAT MAKES A GAMER? FOR A LONG TIME, THIS HAS BEEN one of the most important questions, if not the key question, for understanding video game culture. Who is a gamer, and what makes it official? Is it an identity adopted by the individual, or imposed from the outside? Is the gamer a semi-autonomous, community identity, or a target demographic cultivated by multinational corporations? After the events of late 2014, the importance of these questions has multiplied. For all its intangibility—and for all its visible hate and utter lack of accountability—the social media event that was Gamergate was waged under the banner of the gamer. To be a gamer now is to be, at least in part, marked by the color of Gamergate. What makes a gamer, indeed.

Gamergate was a semi-autonomous campaign that appeared online at the end of August 2014, giving a name and a brand to the ongoing harassment of women in games that has been growing louder in visibility and intensity for years. Ostensibly, it arose in reaction to a number of events that aren't worth going into; in reality, it is an extension of the kind of semi-organized harassment and misogynistic hate of the kind that fellow contributors to this volume, Anita Sarkeesian and Zoe Quinn, have been receiving for years. But what is particularly interesting about its guise under Gamergate is that it is in part imagined as a defense of both video games themselves and the gamer—both of whom are imagined as under attack from "feminist bullies," as one partisan journalist wrote. The gamer, according to this mentality, is at risk and needs defending.

In many ways, it makes complete sense that the gamer should be such a closely policed and defended identity. For decades, it has been a shield to hide behind and a banner to unite under. The gamer was, for many, the recognized enthusiast who was given a legitimacy of sorts through the depths of their passion and intensity of their fanaticism. Though video games themselves were often disregarded and belittled by the mainstream press, the gamer identity was a way of taking that denigration and re-routing it into a positive, almost belligerent enthusiasm. Putting on the gamer identity was how an individual was allowed to like video games. It was a recognizable role to play and a way of reclaiming the clichéd signs of the video game fan that were stigmatized—the darkened room, the hypnotic glow of the screen, the junk food, the late obsessive hours. For each pejorative claim of the uselessness of video games, the gamer could present a flip side. Through this lens, the cliché of the gamer's social awkwardness became the myth of the elite gamer's spectacular playing skill. The stereotype of obsessiveness became the way a gamer gained status within the community through their very particular knowledge. The way the gamer served as a stand-in for the troubles of our times, at least for the tabloid press—as slackers and time-wasters—became for the video game community a way of responding to a world that doesn't care to look beneath the surface. The myth of ridicule from the mainstream—the "outside"—fed the burning need for gamers to stick together.

I remember being called a gamer by others long before I ever called myself one. This was during high school in a rural Australian town—already a context full-to-overflowing with tensions of outsider versus insider culture—and it was often by those who were uninterested in games, but who wanted to understand who I was. Small towns in Australia are, I imagine, much like small towns anywhere in the world, where most residents will recognize you at least by sight, if not by name. At the time, I was a nerd of the highest order—not just interested in games, but also the emerging Internet (which, let's not forget, was deeply uncool in its early years), books, and, most damning of all, big band jazz. I played the clarinet, and I played video games. Carrying a game cartridge from the only video store in town over the ten-minute walk home made me visible. My strange interests painted an unsatisfactory picture at the time of what a boy should be like. Acquaintances could not understand me. But they could understand a gamer. And so to them, I became one.

On a personal level, the term itself was never satisfactory. Later, at university, I developed a deep love of film—in many ways deeper than my appreciation of video games, even—and yet I never felt the urge to call myself a cinephile, let alone a film buff. "Gamer," to me, even high school me, fed into too many associations and preconceptions that I didn't like. I liked to think of myself as more than just the sum of my media interests.

The irony of this is, of course, that there were few reasons to exclude myself from the identity on a demographic basis. Nothing about my gender, sexuality, race, or class excludes me from the stereotypical gamer identity. As a straight, cis, white, middle class man, I had unencumbered access to the gamer identity when—though I did not realize it at the time—others did not. Maleness in particular is the invisible trait of the gamer that has been cultivated for decades.

The gamer identity is not the community-led, organic label that romanticized visions of video game culture would have you believe. Though it has served as a standard to bear against mainstream culture, it is in fact more of a fabrication of marketing departments than one of everyday people. The gamer did not emerge slowly to help give voice to disempowered communities. It was created.

Taken in its simplest, most basic form, a video game is a creative application of computer technology. This is something that not many people think about. Other media have a material basis that sets them apart (film, for example, is named after the celluloid material that underpins the form), but video games are simply made from computers, a medium that also powers scientific calculations, word processing, and the Internet. So the video game began its life as part of computer culture, as creative experiments with new technologies. A number of these early experiments were in the masculine context of university computing labs, such as the MIT's Tech Model Railroad Club, who in February 1962 created *Spacewar!*, one of the first ever video games. The Model Railroad Club's image fulfilled the stereotype of the male nerd with an overwhelming interest in the technical world, boasting members with nicknames like "Slug" and "Shag." Women have always been there for the creation of computing technology—and yes, video game technology, too—but their contributions have often been deliberately made invisible. Jean Jennings was one of five women who programmed ENIAC, the first general purpose computer, and although she was invited—required, even—to give a demonstration to the national press for its launch, neither she nor the four other women programmers involved were invited to the reception afterward. "We felt as if we had been playing parts in a fascinating movie that suddenly took a bad turn," Jennings wrote in her autobiography. "We had worked like dogs for two weeks to produce something really spectacular and then were written out of the script." Other women were early pioneers of the video game: Carol Shaw worked at Atari and then Activision throughout the 1970s and early '80s, creating *River Raid* for the Atari 2600 in 1982, while Dona Bailey worked with Ed Logg to program the amazing arcade game *Centipede* in 1981. In 1979, Roberta Williams, with her husband Ken, founded a company that would become Sierra On-Line, one of the most influential video game developers of the '80s. Women have always played video games, too. Carol Shaw told Polygon in 2013 that when working for Atari, no one spoke about the gender of their players, and it was never assumed, either. "We never really discussed who our target demographic was," said Shaw. "We didn't discuss gender or age."

Yet throughout these early years of video games, something else was going on. Video game culture developed a limited, inward-looking perception of the world that marked game enthusiasts as different from everyone else. Game culture began to separate itself out from technology culture. The product was "the gamer," an identity based on difference and separateness. The gamer was partly related to the geek and the nerd, stereotypes that suggest a monomaniacal interest in the esoteric and the technical. These are potent—and deeply inconsistent—stereotypes that have been wielded with bluntness over the years, both by the media and by technology enthusiasts themselves. The gamer has proven to be just as vague and indistinct a character, with a sense of otherness tied up in video game appreciation as perhaps the only consistent trait. To be a gamer is not just to be interested in video games—it is also to feel separate and to stand apart in one way or another. The gamer identity is therefore at least in part negatively defined. What the gamer is not is almost as important as what the gamer is.

In his book *Computer Games and the Social Imaginary*, Graeme Kirkpatrick argues that the gamer identity became fully realized with the invention or discovery of the concept of "gameplay." Gameplay is a somewhat ineffable term for describing the gameliness of a game; it is a quality that only the most experienced player, the true gamer, is best placed to identify. A gamer's game possesses good gameplay above all else, as distinct from and sometimes in opposition to a game's narrative, representational, or technical elements. This noticeable transformation occurred at some point in the '80s. Kirkpatrick identifies March 1985 as the moment the term gameplay entered the lexicon of British video game magazines in particular. With the discovery of gameplay, the gamer identity was more codified. The development of taste led to the development of identity. Again, this was partly a question of what the gamer was not, and it is reflected in Kirkpatrick's analysis of what seems to be the imagined readership of these British magazines. The gamer was not interested in technology for technology's sake. The gamer was not a parent looking to research educational video games for their children to play. And according to the picture painted by game magazines and their advertisers, the gamer was usually not a woman.

It was only five years earlier that a video game had been created specifically for women for what was likely the first time. Toru Iwatani, a designer working for Namco, thought the video game arcades of the era were offputtingly masculine. If the advertisements for Atari's first arcade machine, *Computer Space*, are anything to go by, he was on to something: the adverts, a paean to 1970s chic, feature a Farrah Fawcett blow-waved woman with her underwear visible through a sheer white dress, leaning seductively against the machine. In an attempt to break down this male-dominated culture, Iwatani created a game called *Puc-Man*. It was a game that he thought might attract women and couples to the arcade. Iwatani's reasoning? "When I imagined what women enjoy, the image of them eating cakes and desserts came to mind, so I used 'eating' as a keyword," he told Eurogamer in 2010. "When I did research with this keyword I came across the image of a pizza with a slice taken out of it and had that eureka moment." Condescending as they were, Iwatani's actions reveal the invisible masculinity inherent in popular games of the era.

There's a naïve optimism to video game advertising of the early 1980s that contains a kind of universalism not yet divided by gender. Women—particularly girls—feature in advertisements for *Millipede* and the Atari 2600. In an advertisement for *Bandits* by Sirius in the September 1983 issue of *Electronic Games Magazine*, a cartoon girl defiantly tells a military man, "Girls like to play video games too!" She then defeats an invading alien force before telling "Captain Star" to "eat your heart out!"

Beyond the mid-'80s things shift dramatically. In 1998, an ad for the original PlayStation places a couple in a movie theatre. She's bothering him, trying to get his attention from the film. Crash Bandicoot as the usher appears to berate the man, mocking him for being "totally whipped." Then Lara Croft suddenly appears next to the man. "Would you rather be at home shooting a bazooka, or watching a chick flick?" asks Crash. Cut to the next scene and the man and Lara Croft are playing their PlayStation together at home while the man's partner cries to be let in at the front door. Another ad, this time for the 2005 racing game *Juiced*, sees two men playing the game in their car. They realize their controllers are altering not just the video game, but also the clothes of a woman on the pavement outside. The men giggle as they use their controllers to strip the clearly horrified woman naked. The industry's imagined target demographic for the video game is by this point utterly clear, not just in advertising, but in the branding of video game consoles themselves—GameBoy, anyone? This became a self-fulfilling prophesy. Who plays video games? Young men and boys, such marketing claims. So who are video games made for and aimed at? Young men and boys. As a result, by the late 2000s, efforts to deliberately target women players seemed only to be possible through absurdly demeaning flourishes of the color pink, or with the "girls only" branding of Ubisoft's *Imagine* series (2007–2013). The gendered gamer identity helped demarcate the gamer as a targetable demographic for business. People always exist in multiple forms of identity simultaneously. I can be a man and a musician and a writer and a scholar all at once, for example. One could very easily be a woman and a gamer simultaneously, or queer and a gamer, or African and a gamer. Yet for the marketers, journalists, and developers who helped shape the world of video games in the '80s and '90s, only a few traits defined the gamer. The most immovable of these was that he was a man.

Unsurprisingly, shaped by the weight of decades of gendered and sexualized design and marketing, the gamer identity is deeply bound up in assumptions and performances of gender and sexuality. To be a gamer is to signal a great many things, not all of which are about the actual playing of video games. For her essay, "Do You Identify As A Gamer? Gender, Race, Sexuality, and Gamer Identity," Adrienne Shaw interviewed a selection of non-heterosexual, non-male, and not solely White or Anglo people who played video games. On the basis of her interviews, Shaw concluded there was "a definite correlation between gender and gamer identity." Put simply: men were much more likely to identify as gamers, regardless of the actual quantity of video game playing in their lives. Other studies have also suggested that women tend to underestimate the amount of time they spend playing video games—and like Shaw's study, Simeon Yates and Karen Littleton's 1999 investigation, "Understanding Computer Game Cultures: A Situated Approach," concludes that women are also less likely to adopt the gamer identity. This is not to say that no woman ever has identified as a gamer—this is patently untrue—but rather that through decades of built-up pressure from marketing, branding, culture, and even the games themselves, women are less likely to take on the gamer moniker.

Despite all this, a substantial demographic variety has always been present in the range of people who play video games. Time and time again, each study has proven that not only a substantial number of women play video games, but that they play video games just as seriously and with the same dedication as their male counterparts. In late 2014, a small stir was created when the ESA released its latest survey of American gaming habits and announced that adult women represent a much bigger proportion of the game-playing population than teenage boys. Yet this has been the trend in video game demographic surveys for years for anyone who has been paying attention. The predictable response—"What kind of games do they really play, though—are they really gamers?"—says all you need to know about this ongoing demographic shift. The insinuated criteria of "real" video games is wholly contingent on identity (i.e. a real gamer shouldn't play *Candy Crush*). In a way, what we are seeing with these kinds of insinuations is the replaying of gendered debates that have been going on for centuries.

The gamer identity has also stagnated. Perhaps the biggest shift for the industry since the end of the arcade era occurred when Nintendo released the Wii in 2006. Almost overnight, the mimetic and accessible nature of the Wii seemed to open up video games to mainstream audiences. This is the narrative we hear about, anyway—the actual story is a bit more complex, given that people who are not straight white men have clearly been playing and making video games since their inception. Perhaps it is more accurate to say that after years of ignoring them, the video game industry could now allow itself to make games that acknowledged the existence of a wide variety of gamers. We suddenly saw Nintendo ads featuring women, the elderly, and the non-white. This was not the discovery of video games by a new demographic, but the video game industry authorizing new stories to be told about its players. The image of gaming was changing—and in the case of the Nintendo Wii ads, it was changing quite literally. This change has only been amplified in the years since, with the social gaming boon on Facebook and smartphones that is stereotypically associated with women and other nontraditional gamer groups.

The gamer—an identity still tied up in ideas of otherness, outsider status, and masculinity—quite quickly started to become an irrelevant concept in the late 2000s. There was nothing exclusive about the Nintendo Wii. There was nothing about *Candy Crush* that signified a special insider culture. The gamer identity was not required to explain a player's enthusiasm; this was self-explanatory—video games were now in the mainstream eye.

When the playing of video games moved beyond the niche the industry had always targeted, the gamer identity did not adapt. It remained uniformly stagnant and immobile. As a defensive, negatively defined concept, it was simply not fluid enough to apply to a new broad spectrum of people. It could not meaningfully contain *Candy Crush* players, *Proteus* players, and *Call of Duty* players simultaneously. When video games changed, the gamer identity failed to stretch, and so it has been broken.

We have also seen a video game press—so long allowed to court a male audience—undergo a number of shifts. There has been an increase in the visibility of traditionally marginalized groups—such as women—among game journalists. Just as women have always made and played video games, women have always written about them, too, like Joyce Worley, one of the co-founders of *Electronic Games*, the first video game magazine. Today, the boys club of the 1990s magazine era has become a different online criticism sphere populated by writers like Leigh Alexander, Patricia Hernandez, Cara Ellison, Lana Polansky, Maddy Myers, Jenn Frank, and Keza McDonald. Now more than ever, video game journalists are more interested in issues of representation, equality, and feminism, too. The stratospheric rise of a critic like Anita Sarkeesian is hugely significant, but must also be seen in context as merely the brightest star in an array of critics more vocally attacking sexism, racism, homophobia, transphobia, and ableism in video games than ever before. Video game criticism has shifted in a noticeably progressive direction, even if the games themselves have been slow to keep up.

In this context, what are we to make of Gamergate? On the evidence of its sustained and ferocious attack on women in games, what we are seeing is the end of the gamer and the viciousness that accompanies the death of an identity. The gamer identity has been broken. It no longer has a niche to call home, and so it reaches out inarticulately at invented and easy targets instead. That the supposed *raison d'être* of Gamergate was corruption and bias in the video game media makes complete sense; this is just another way of expressing confusion about why games the traditional gamer does not understand are successful, like Zoe Quinn's *Depression Quest*, a video game about an emotional topic, made by a woman. That the game is made in Twine is yet another point of confusion for the traditional gamer, since Twine, being a text-based platform, does not stimulate the traditional taste for gameplay.

The gamer identity is under assault, and so it should be. It is also tied up in complex notions of consumption and capitalism: the gamer is someone who purchases video games, above anything else. The cries of Gamergate that claim consumers have been needlessly and wantonly attacked illustrate this nakedly. The gamer is, among other things, an identity that has for decades been framed at the financial heart of an entire creative industry. The gamer community has been told the consumer is always right—and that the consumer is mostly male. The "consumer king" gamer, as developer and writer Matthew Burns puts it, will continue to be targeted and exploited while their profitability as a demographic outweighs their toxicity, but the traditional gamer identity is now culturally irrelevant. The battles to make safe spaces for different video game cultures are long and they are resisted tempestuously. Given the extremes to which this conflict has been taken, I don't use the word "battle" lightly; with now-numerous women run out of their homes and threatened with rape and death, perhaps "war" is more appropriate. Through the pain and suffering of people who have their friendships, personal lives, and professions on the line, things continue to improve. The myth of the male gamer, once at the center of an entire industry, has been destabilized and replaced with a more complex picture. The result has been a palpable progressive shift.

This shift is precisely the root of the increasingly violent hostility of Gamergate. The hysterical fits of those inculcated at the heart of male gamer culture might on the surface be claimed as crusades for journalistic integrity, or a defense against falsehoods, but—along with a mix of the hatred of women and an expansive bigotry thrown in for good measure—what is actually going on is an attempt to retain hegemony. Make no mistake: the death threats, the bomb threats, and all the words of violence on social media are manifestations of the exertion of power in the name of male-gamer orthodoxy. It is an orthodoxy that has already begun to disappear.

Gamergate represented the moment that gamers realized their own irrelevance. This was a cold wind a long time coming. For decades, the gamer was told by advertising, branding, and, most importantly, by gamers themselves, that they were the lords of their domain. The outside world may have contempt for us, the gamer imagined, but in here we rule. We may continue to ask what makes a gamer into the future, but what we have seen so clearly in late 2014 is what unmakes a gamer.

Video games are for everyone today. I mean this in a destructive way. To read the other side of the same statement—especially if you align yourself with the old-school gamer identity—video games are no longer for you. You do not get to own them. No single group gets to own them anymore. On some level, the grim individuals who are self-centered and myopic enough to be upset at the prospect of having to share their medium are absolutely right. They have astutely and correctly identified what is going on here. Their toys are being taken away, their treehouses are being boarded up. Video games now live in the world and there is no going back.

I am convinced this marks the end. We are finished here. From now on, there are no more gamers, only players.

Dan Golding is a video game, music, and film critic and academic based in Melbourne, Australia.

The Joy of Virtual Violence

CARA ELLISON & BRENDAN KEOGH

Violence has always been a core mechanic in video games, leading to an endless debate on whether or not violent video games encourage violent behavior in real life. In this essay, Cara Ellison and Brendan Keogh defer the question of right or wrong to instead focus on "the why": Why is violence so ubiquitous in games? And why is it so much fun? Their conversation draws on everything from John Milton to John Romero, shedding light both on our enjoyment of violence in games and on the forces that control how exactly it is portrayed.

Dear Brendan,

Once upon a time, a friend wrote me an email. In it, she explained her worry that people were talking about the violent room-clearing assassination game *Hotline Miami* in adoring terms, rather than thinking about what video game violence does to us.

I love *Hotline Miami*. But I also think games are too violent. How can we reconcile the two? Is there something wrong with me? What about me is attracted to this aspect of games?

I've had a long time to think about it. I've become wiser. And I've read people smarter than me talk about the matter. And I think I understand myself better now.

Let me elaborate.

I read *Paradise Lost* when I was much too young to understand it. *Paradise Lost* is John Milton's overlong rhetorical poem about the politics of heaven and hell; about the creation of hell in opposition to heaven, and Satan's role in it. At the time I read it, when the descriptions of God casting out Satan and the image of Satan's wings being burned off were fresh in my mind, I was puzzled at the injustice portrayed there. I thought Milton was sympathizing, like the Rolling Stones, with the Devil.

Isn't John Milton a Christian? I thought, reading as a fully clueless agnostic. Doesn't he value the moral teachings of God? God seems insufferable in this poem. A dismissive patriarch. A boring moralizer.

This book is teaching me to sympathize with Satan, I decided. Satan's charisma, the way he questions his ruler, his grandstanding speeches, his love of destruction, his sultry burnt wing-stubs a symbol of his mistreatment—he's beautiful. He's fascinating.

Also, Satan's right: it's fun to destroy.

I worried about myself for a while, sympathizing with a figure that my long-abandoned Christian upbringing had taught me was the root of all human failure. For a while, I wondered if the reason I liked *Doom* and *Dungeon Keeper* was because I was really sympathizing with the Devil.

But it didn't take long for me to recognize the device. I recognized that what was being said was that human beings are the sons and daughters of both creation and destruction. We love to do both. After all, isn't sex the creation of love and children? And war is the destruction of lives. And neither will ever end until the earth explodes.

It was several years before I thought about this again, in which time I had become known for critiquing games professionally. Brenda Romero, the doyenne of game designers, pointed me toward her husband's blog post, called "Tidiness Theory." In it, John Romero, the co-creator of *Doom*, which is one of the most influential first-person shooters of all time, outlines his theory that all games are about cleaning up. They are about order, he argues:

> In *Pac-Man*, the mess is the maze full of dots. You need to clean them up to achieve your goal of cleanliness. In *Space Invaders*, the aliens are the mess. Clean them up

and you reach your goal. In *Bejeweled* you are presented with a messy screen of jewels. Arrange them in groups of matching threes and you clean it up, one match at a time. Chess? Clean the board of your opponent's pieces, specifically his king. The ancient game of Go? Same mechanic.

Romero argues that his game *Doom*—essentially a game about violently and bloodily killing horrific monsters and mutated beings—is just about making order from chaos. About cleaning levels. He concludes, "This tidiness theory, this instinct toward Order rather than Chaos, may be evolutionary and part of our DNA."

Are violent games a way of asking a player to clean up a mess the designer made on purpose? Are violent games a pursuit of order?

Yours murderously,
Cara

× × ×

Dear Cara,

Thank you for your letter. What a complicated topic you've dragged us into here! Trying to navigate a conversation about violence in video games is so difficult. On one side you have those who would use video games as an easy scapegoat for all of society's ills rather than consider more deeply ingrained issues such as insufficient welfare systems or ineffective gun laws. On the other side you have those willing to defend video games against any and all accusations, no matter how sound they are. Trying to find a nuanced position between these two extremes is like trying to walk a tightrope.

Why are video games so violent in the first place? Why do we have—why have we always had—so many video games about shooting and punching monsters and bad guys, but so few about, say, going on a summer road trip with your friends? Or some kind of British romantic comedy? Having to choose between Collin Firth and Hugh Grant sounds like a far more challenging dilemma than anything I faced in *Fallout 3*!

I really like Romero's idea of games as cleaning up, of finding order, but I'm not sure it goes quite far enough. I played a lot of *Doom* when I was far too young to be playing a game like *Doom* (my mum would write a signed note that I would take to the lady at the video store so she would let me rent out the Super Nintendo cart. In hindsight

I'm not sure that was actually legal). Apart from the abject terror of realizing enemies I couldn't see could still hurt me, what I remember most is being fascinated by how the corpses of the zombies and demons that I blew away never disappeared. They just sat there, scattered through the halls as I walked back and forth past them until I went to the next stage.

In a way that might be disturbing, I really liked that permanence, that ability to see my performance of *Doom* inscribed on the virtual space. I could walk back through the space and see where I blasted that imp or squished that zombie under a door. In more recent violent video games, like *Hotline Miami*, this gets even more detailed. I can see where I shot that guy through a window and he's now splayed out, broken and bloodied, surrounded by broken glass; and where I warped another guy's back with a swing of a golf club. I don't think it is simply ordering these spaces that is so satisfying, but personalizing them with my performance.

Which points at a weird paradox, I think. Destroying and creating are two sides of one coin. I destroy these people and monsters and environments, and I create a visible rendition of my own violent performance of the game. I think this describes most if not all games: the player pokes their fingers into this static and stable thing, messes it up, and in that process of messing it up creates a particularly personal performance. Destroying and creating are a single act.

And that, I think, points to why violence often seems like the default choice for so many video games. It allows outward, directed actions. Physically violent acts have a clear output from one body and a visible input on another. You do something and you get to see the results of that something clearly and immediately. It's not that violence is the best way to manifest the dual act of destruction and creation that play feeds on, it's that violence is the easiest way to achieve it.

But that doesn't make it any less enjoyable, does it? I still thoroughly enjoy a game like *Hotline Miami* or *Doom* today as much as I did as a kid. My lounge-room is full of incredibly violent games where men shoot or stab or punch other men or manly demons or manly robots or manly aliens. As a Western, white, middle-class male that grew up in the '90s, I'm exactly the audience that the creators of these violent games were (and still are) trying to target. As critical of these games as I sometimes am, there's no denying that I still enjoy playing them, and I am not sure how to feel about that.

Where do you think this comes from, this finding of pleasure in violent acts?

Yours bloodily,
Brendan

× × ×

Brendan,

You say, "Destroying and creating are a single act." This reminds me of the way the *Far Cry* series treats environments simply as places to be cleansed of enemies (often enemies explicitly coded as other or foreign to the player), then asks the player to collect and upgrade things for themselves. In a way, this is destroying and creating (oneself), but it's explicitly a colonial narrative: one where the player knows best, the one where the player is ordering things by destroying, one where the consumption of the environment is self-improvement.

This is incredibly sinister. I don't know if games are teaching us to think killing is necessary, but they are tapping into something in us. An instantaneous reaction, followed by a dramatic image or animation in reward flips a switch in me. This is complemented by the idea of collection and upgrade. Is it purely the pretty colors? The pretty things? Is it the very idea of possession, not only of one's environment, but also of an inordinate amount of self-control? Perhaps it is something to do with survival. Are violent images pleasurable to experience, because they tell us we are surviving?

Yours flailingly,
Cara

× × ×

Cara,

I think the colonial narrative you've picked up on is so telling. So many video games, in particular Western ones, are about the lone hero man marching into a strange, foreign land to both order and destroy with a single swipe, not unlike the colonialists through the centuries who have birthed nations through the destruction of countless indigenous cultures.

There is definitely something phenomenological about the virtual act of killing. It feels good. In a well-designed video game, a violent act is crisp, crunchy, meaty, or chunky. The rumble of the controller, the machine-gun fire, and the *splat!* of some enemy's head like a ripe melon all feel undeniably good. I still don't know if it is okay that it feels good, but it certainly does.

But this is also true of nonviolent acts in video games: the elastic bounce of the ball against the pegs in *Peggle*, or the screeching of tires in *Mario Kart*. These games all feel really good without needing to be gratuitously violent. So it's violence, to be sure, but not just violence.

Ultimately, the reason why we have so many violent video games is cultural, and so is the reason why violence has come to be valued as the most significant way of engaging with them. One only has to look at the short history of the medium to see this. So many video games were spawned straight out of the military-entertainment complex. They were hacked out on room-size computers by students attending military-affiliated universities in the decades of the Cold War. Games like *Spacewar!* and *Missile Command* perpetuate not just the anxieties of that time, but the values and tastes of those young men that created them.

This is why video games fit so neatly into colonial narratives: they come from the same powerful demographic of the same culture. Post-Enlightenment Western men have been taught to value power, autonomy, and freedom as things that are owed to them, and to dominate all those deemed lesser in order to claim these. It has become the Manifest Destiny of the playable character to march into a world and to bend it, violently, to *his* will. I don't think this is a deliberate or intentional transferral of values, but an inevitable one. The institutions and people who shaped the form at its inception endowed it with a core value: empowerment through violence.

I personally don't mind the existence of violent video games any more than I mind the existence of violent films or novels, and I don't think they are any more likely to create murderers or destroy society. Such claims are always so reductive as to almost certainly be a smoke screen for some other agenda (such as not wanting to talk about lax gun laws, for instance). But I do think it's crucial—if we are going to argue that video games are meaningful and culturally significant—to be responsible and critical of the kinds of violence we value, explore, and perpetuate. Too often, the violence most valued in video games is a militarized, masculine, and colonial one.

But to wrap this up, I'm interested to hear what other kinds of violence you think video games might be capable of? Are there games that use violence for more than the empowered gratification of a young and male target demographic? What interesting uses of violence in video games have you seen?

Yours viciously,
Brendan

× × ×

Hi Brendan,

It's interesting that you say that Western men have been taught to value certain things—power, autonomy, and freedom—because these are exactly the things that *Bioshock*, for example, ultimately fails to critique. The mechanics of the game are dictated by the player's ability to perpetrate violence within the framework of the levels and a Randian narrative that is proposed as a pursuit of "power, autonomy, and freedom." This is the straitjacket of masculinity—often men are culturally conditioned to perceive that the only way they can respond to their environment is through anger and violence, instead of by expressing emotions or by talking about problems. By the end of the game, at the twist of the story, the player is told that he or she has been a slave to the game's violent narrative and a pawn all along. Then the player is given a choice, which isn't a choice at all. It's something that is meant to be outside the violent narrative. It's supposed to offer "freedom of choice," but of course there's no real choice: it's kill the final boss or have nothing happen at all. That is the only way you can express yourself. Even if the player never wants to be violent, there is no choice in *Bioshock*, because that's how you gain satisfaction from your environment. There is no option to talk. There is no option to do anything but bludgeon a man to death.

But you're right that other games do experiment with violence in other ways. merritt kopas' *Consensual Torture Simulator* is a text game that allows the player to examine what consensual violence toward a sexual partner might be like. The player considers at each option that they are injuring someone else for mutual pleasure. This is emotionally difficult, even if only expressed through text hyperlink options. Even though the game doesn't convey graphic violence, the violence ends up having an impact on the player.

In a similar manner, the text game *Cyberqueen* by the artist Porpentine is about the violence perpetrated on the player character by a brutal cyberpunk AI character. It describes the control the AI character has over your body, violating it and attempting to destroy it. The violence is conveyed in an erotic manner, having the player imagine the dominance of the AI over the player's body, describing the liquids and feelings of having to give up bodily autonomy to her, the Cyberqueen. The text is navigated through hyperlinks, but transitions to new passages are often delayed, making you wait for your fate, making you wonder what will happen to you. It is tantalizing and horrifying at the same time, but it reveals that games are interested in what happens to the player's perception of violence when it is perpetrated upon them.

The educational game *Sweatshop HD* is a game I worked on as an assistant producer at Littleloud, where we used a tower defense-style game to illustrate how oppressive sweatshop conditions endanger and exploit child workers and expose them to violence, merely in pursuit of cheap fashion. Not spending enough money on fire equipment or on maintenance means that often the workers would come to a violent, bloody end. The graphics are cartoony, unlike highly realistic and bloody first-person games like *Call of Duty* or *Bioshock*, and yet Apple deemed a sweatshop theme too offensive to keep on the App Store.

What is interesting is that Porpentine's and merritt kopas' games were distributed directly from the artists to players over the Internet. *Cyberqueen* is free and *Consensual Torture Simulator* is available for a small fee. *Sweatshop HD* was funded by Channel Four and was supposed to be sold on the App Store. But as soon as a large company like Apple was involved, it became politicized.

We need to ask why big companies refuse to fund, host, and distribute games that ask us incisive questions about our already violent world. Can we afford to ignore the fact that a game like *Sweatshop HD* is dropped while at the same time large publishers are routinely paying arms manufacturers licence fees so first-person shooters can feature their weapons?

It's clear that some parts of our industry are doing as much as they can to explore these issues. It's the rest of the world that needs to catch up.

Yours violently, but in hope,
Cara

Cara Ellison is a journalist and video game critic. She writes regularly for The Guardian, Rock Paper Shotgun, *and* Kotaku. *She is also the creator of* Sacrilege, *a Twine game about sex and relationships. Brendan Keogh is a critic and PhD candidate at RMIT University, Melbourne, where he researches and writes about the phenomenological and textual entwinings of players and video games*

The Squalid Grace of *Flappy Bird*

IAN BOGOST

The story of *Flappy Bird* is one of the oddest to come out of video game culture. Created for smartphones by a single developer in Vietnam, this absurdly simple game became a sudden worldwide sensation in 2014. It made its creator Dong Nguyen a wealthy man, but also a remorseful one. The game, Nguyen said, was too addictive, and he himself was getting way too much attention for his taste. So in a surprise move, he pulled his game from sale at the height of its popularity. *Flappy Bird* is minimalistic, to say the least, yet according to Ian Bogost it offers new and unprecedented insight into what makes all players tick.

GAMES ARE GROTESQUE.

I'm not talking about games like *Grand Theft Auto* or *Manhunt*, games whose subjects are moral turpitude, games that that ask players to murder, maim, or destroy. I mean games in general, the form we call "games." Games are gross, revolting heaps of arbitrary anguish. Games are encounters with squalor. You don't play a game to experience an idea so much as you do so in an attempt to get a broken machine to work again.

In this way, games are different from other media. Sure, a movie, book, or painting can depict squalor, can attune us to the agony of misfortune. But unlike film and literature, games do not primarily depict human events and tell stories. And unlike sports, games do not primarily showcase physical prowess. We don't watch or read games like we do novels, movies, and paintings, nor do we perform them like we might dance or throw a football or Frisbee. We do something in between with games. Yes, we "play" games like we do sports, and yes, games bear "meaning" as do the fine and plastic arts. But something else is at work. Games are devices we operate.

Sometimes that operation simulates piloting a mecha, a pro athlete, or a space marine, but more frequently it entails mundane activities, like moving cards between stacks in *Klondike Solitaire*, swapping adjacent gems in *Bejeweled*, or directing a circular, discarnate maw in *Pac-Man*. Some machinery is fantastic, but most is ordinary, forgettable, broken.

If you look past the familiar shimmer of *Super Mario Bros.* and Super Bowl Sunday, there in the middle you will find the unsung paragons of gaming: games like chess, backgammon, tic-tac-toe, crosswords, Go, Dots and Boxes, Monopoly, Candy Land, and Sorry! These are games that frustrate more than they titillate, because operating them involves minimal effort yet considerable misery. It's not the misery of boredom or stupidity, but the misery of repetition. The misery of knowing what you want to accomplish but not being able to, whether thanks to the plodding pace of a child's board game, or the bottomless strategic depth of a folk classic. Football yields its beauty through the practiced triumph of the human body and will over circumstance. Sorry! delivers only the stupid, gratuitous anguish caused by our decision to play it in the first place.

Every now and then a game comes along that forces us to admit the inconvenient truth of games. Recently, we have been graced with one—a free mobile throwaway called *Flappy Bird*. The game was first released last summer, but as the year wound down it experienced an unexpected surge in popularity. By the start of 2014, it had nested itself at the top of the Apple App Store free charts.

Flappy Bird is a stupid game. You control a bird so cute it signals deformity. Tapping the screen causes the bird to flap, making it rise slightly before quickly falling. The game asks only that you pilot the bird through narrow passageways between two green, *Super Mario*-style pipes that issue from the top and bottom of the screen. A point is awarded for every pipe you pass. But touch anything and the cute bird tumbles beak-first into the ground. Game over.

Flappy Bird is a perversely, oppressively difficult game. Scoring even a single point takes most players a considerable number of runs. After my first hour, I'd managed a high score of two. Many, many hours of play later, my high score is now 32, a feat that has earned me the game's gold medal (whatever that means).

There is a tradition of such super-difficult games, sometimes called masocore among the video game savvy. Masocore games are normally characterized by trial and error gameplay, but split up into levels or areas to create a sense of overall progress. Commercial blockbusters like *Mega Man* inaugurated the category (even if the term appeared long after Capcom first released that title in 1987), and more recent independent titles like *I Wanna Be The Guy* and *Super Meat Boy* have further explored the idea of intense difficulty as a primary aesthetic. Combined with repetition and progression, the intense difficulty of masocore games often produces a feeling of profound accomplishment, an underdog's victory in the dorky medium of underdogs themselves, 2D platformer video games.

Even though *Flappy Bird* borrows from the same platformer tradition, it's no masocore game. For one part, masocore is more of an aesthetic community than it is a material aesthetic. Like the poetry and painting that emerged from the Pre-Raphaelite Brotherhood, masocore games arise from a dedication to a particular kind of play experience, or perhaps even more to a disgust with the rise of facile "everybody wins" games.

Flappy Bird is not difficult because it wants to oppose any regime in particular, a fact made flesh by its deployment on the mobile platforms that have only accelerated casual play. *Flappy Bird* is not difficult to challenge you, nor even to teach the institution of video games a thing or two. Rather, *Flappy Bird* is difficult because that's how it is. It is a game that is indifferent, like an iron gate rusted shut, like the ice that shuts down a city. It's not hard for the sake of your experience; it's just hard because that's the way it is. Where masocore games want nothing more than to please their players with pain and humiliation (thus their appropriation of the term "masochism"), *Flappy Bird* just exists. It wants nothing and expects even less.

The game seems to have come out of nowhere. It was created by a lone, twenty-nine-year-old Vietnamese developer named Dong Nguyen, who has mostly denied requests for press interviews after the explosive success of his game. Nguyen operates under the shingle .GEARS, which has released several other games with a similar avant-pixel aesthetic and simple gameplay. While tech press outlets accustomed to megalomaniac entrepreneurs motivated only by fame and wealth have reframed the creator's timidity as "mystery," Nguyen's own words likely explain the situation more accurately: "The popularity could be my luck."

Nguyen's status as an outsider artist may be the key to the game's deftly indifferent design, even if it can't explain its success. .GEARS' earlier games are much rougher and less refined than *Flappy Bird*. In *Shuriken Block*, the player taps on the screen to deflect throwing stars that would otherwise lodge in the heads of a row of cute samurai. A correct tap issued more quickly yields more points than one at the last minute. But an observant player can simply turn the game into a joke, tapping constantly at the top of the screen to achieve as high a score as patience affords. In *Super Ball Juggling*, the player taps the right and left sides of the screen to individually control two soccer players juggling balls that rise to different heights with each bounce. After a few singular practice juggles, balls appear simultaneously on both sides, and the player must struggle against the absence of a continuous rhythm to perform well at the game.

But rather than improving upon these and other game design techniques, *Flappy Bird* actually regresses, offering fewer rather than more crutches for either novice or expert play. It even withdraws from the gentler onboarding of *Super Ball Juggling*.

Contemporary design practice would recommend an "easy" first pipe sequence to get the player started, perhaps a few pipes positioned at the bird's initial position, or with wider openings for easier passage. More difficult maneuvers, such as quick shifts from high to low pipe openings, would be reserved for later in the game, with difficulty ramping up as the player demonstrates increased expertise.

But *Flappy Bird* offers no such scaffolding. Instead, every pipe and every point is completely identical: randomly positioned but uniform in every other way. A game of *Flappy Bird* is a series of identical maneuvers, one after the other. All you have to do is keep responding to them, a task made possible by the game's predictable and utterly reasonable interactions. Just keep flapping.

This indifference to player capacity and expectation makes *Flappy Bird* a particularly earnest device to operate. Many players have expressed astonishment and distress at their simultaneous hatred for and commitment to the game—"I Hate *Flappy Bird*, But I Can't Stop Playing It"—essentially concluding that the game is just another addictive trifle, a curiosity that cannot be understood despite spilling ink in the effort. Meanwhile, the tech press continues its tendency to present business as aesthetics, limiting its coverage of *Flappy Bird* to the game's viral success. It also explains the gold-rush insurgence of copycat games like *Ironpants,* which mistake *Flappy Bird*'s surprise success for a predictable design pattern rather than a confluence of accidents.

In game design circles, we sometimes wax poetic about the elegance and simplicity of a design, the way complex emergent behaviors can arise from simple rules and structures. This is why game designers tend to love games like Go and *Tetris*—tiny flowers that betray their simplicity by divulging endless fractal blossoms.

But in fetishizing simplicity, we also mistake the elegance of design for beauty. For Go and *Tetris* are likewise ghastly, erupting stones and tetrominoes endlessly, failing to relent in their desire to overtake us. The games we find ourselves ever more devoted to are often also the ones that care very little for our experience of them. This is the devotion to material indifference. To understand *Flappy Bird*, we must accept the premise that games are squalid, rusty machinery, which we operate in spite of them and ourselves. What we appreciate about *Flappy Bird* is not the details of its design, but the fact that it embodies them with such unflappable nonchalance. The best games are not for us (or for anyone), but instead strive to be what they are as much as possible. From this indifference emanates a strange squalor that we can appreciate as beauty.

Let me explain what I mean. The day before I fell prey to the *Flappy Bird* phenomenon, I spent two hours attempting to fix a bathroom cabinet drawer pull that was coming unattached on one side, hanging despondently at the bottom of the vanity. I detached the hardware and confirmed that the handle happily accepted the machine screw into its threads, but somehow the two weren't meshing when set in the drawer front. I drilled to widen the hole through which the screw passed, noting that the screw seemed to require a precise orthogonal orientation to thread properly. I swapped both orientations and screws, thinking that I'd achieve a more accurate alignment. I deployed penlights and vice grips. My family began receding ever further into the house, aware of the dark shadow that grew from the bathroom, where an oiled bronze drawer pull was siphoning out vitality from our residence and, perhaps, from the universe itself.

A commitment to *Flappy Bird* is akin to the sensation you have after two hours splayed on the floor of your bathroom, when you still haven't managed to reattach a cabinet pull that somehow won't stay attached to the drawer, even though the hardware happily accepts the machine screw when you hold both pieces in your hand. Emergence is also chaos, and its charm is the beauty of a universe that could have been nothing, but turned out to be something instead. That something is both revolting and divine, and we cheat ourselves when we take the one alone without the other.

Compared to other games, *Flappy Bird* offers a more ardent take on unconcern. Instead of relying on the exploding permutational space of a few easily memorizable gestures, it relies on the cold fury of sheer repetition instead. Like Candy Land, that scourge of preschools and pediatrician offices, *Flappy Bird* demands only that you do the same thing again and again, until something else interrupts you—and then it removes the only guarantee of interruption Candy Land affords, that of a certain victory and an excuse to put the game away.

And not for lack of other options, either. *Flappy Bird* is hardly a new design—it follows in the footsteps of a genre now known as the "endless runner," named after the 2009 mobile hit *Canabalt*, in which players help a man outrun an unseen threat that destroys the city whose rooftops he traverses to escape. *Canabalt* begat similar titles, including the massive hit *Temple Run*, whose sequel was installed over fifty million times in two weeks.

The endless runner itself has a lineage, which *Flappy Bird* likewise spurns. Writing in *The New Yorker* last year, Simon Parkin traced the origins of the genre first to a frequently recreated DOS game with a helicopter in an endless tunnel, and before that to a 1983 Commodore 64 game, *B.C.'s Quest For Tires*, based on the classic caveman comic strip by Johnny Hart. But even three decades ago, *B.C.'s Quest For Tires* offered more sophistication than *Flappy Bird*. The caveman on his stone unicycle must avoid multiple obstacles—he must jump over rocks, duck under trees, avoid rolling stones, and so forth—while enduring regular increases in the speed of progress.

Set in relief against its precursors, *Flappy Bird* seems positively minimalist. The zen garden school of design would encourage us to interpret this choice as more rather than less sophisticated: by removing all unnecessary elements, the purity of the endless runner is revealed. This sounds good on paper, but the experience of *Flappy Bird* betrays it. "Surely something else will happen?" asks the *Flappy Bird* player, over and over. But nothing ever does. This isn't a surplus of design thanks to unadornment, but a brazen opposition to modernist elegance by means of the austere design that tradition holds so dear. This discomfort echoes all throughout the *Flappy Bird* experience. Is it just a bad minimalist runner, or is it purposely disparaging the genre it adopts?

The answer is neither: *Flappy Bird* is not amateurish nor sociopathic. Instead, it is something more unusual. It is earnest. It is exactly what it is, and it is unapologetic. Not even unapologetic—aloof. Impervious. Like a meteorite that crashed through a desert motel lobby, hot and small and unaware.

Playing *Flappy Bird* is like fixing an unfixable drawer pull, one that will never reattach correctly, one that you know will never do, but persisting in the face of such torpor nevertheless. *Flappy Bird* is a condition of the universe, even if it is one that didn't exist until it was hand-crafted by a man who doesn't want to talk about it. It is a condition in the sense of a circumstance, but also in the sense of a blight, sickness, or stain we cannot scrub out but may in time be willing to accept. A stain like our own miserable, tiny existences as players, which we nevertheless believe are more fundamental than the existence of bird flapping games or machine screws or the cold fog rising against the melting snow in the morning. Because the game cares so little for your experience of it, you find yourself ever more devoted to it.

Mere moments after its explosive rise, Dong Nguyen dramatically pulled *Flappy Bird* from the Apple App Store and Google Play, claiming it was too addictive. "I just wanted to create a game that people could enjoy for a few minutes," he told the *Wall Street Journal*. On the one hand, one can't help but admire Nguyen for apparently sacrificing the enormous sums *Flappy Bird* had been earning from advertising (up to $50,000 per day, according to some reports), especially at a time when the biggest mobile and social game companies will do anything to make a buck. But why should Dong Nguyen derive uncomplicated satisfaction from his creation any more than his players should from its operation? Dong Nguyen's error was not in making *Flappy Bird*, but in failing to see it from a creator's perspective as the challenge against reason, decorum, and comfort it truly is.

We like to think of video games as an entertainment medium on the move—a contender to replace (or at least to match) the influence and appeal of literature, film, painting, dance, and sculpture. Video games are a way of presenting ideas and experiences through our most contemporary of vessels: the computer. We may often play games because they allow us to be someone fantastic and unassailable. But games are also ancient, and ancient things teach us humility. Just as often, we play games because they are there to be played, because we want to feel what it's like to play them, and because we are not clever or strong or fast, but because we can move stones on wooden boards or shift cards on cardboard or make a tiny bird flap its wings.

We play games because games are stupid, like drawer pulls are stupid. *Flappy Bird* is a game that accepts that it is stupid. It offers us an example of what it might feel like to conclude that this is enough. That it's enough for games just to be crap in the universe, detritus that we encounter from time to time, and that we might encounter *as* detritus rather than as meaning. That we might stop to manipulate them without motive or reason, like we might turn a smooth rock in our palms before tossing it back into the big ocean, which devours it. For no matter how stupid it is to be a game, it is no less stupid to be a man who plays one.

Ian Bogost is an author, game designer, and professor of interactive computing at the Georgia Institute of Technology.

The Making of *Dust*: Architecture and the Art of Level Design

DAVID JOHNSTON

What makes a room, house, or city block livable? Does the answer have anything in common with what makes it playable? In crafting game worlds—"maps" or "levels," as they are called in the business—a designer creates spaces that on the surface may seem as close to reality as technology allows. In fact, game designers often emphasize the exact opposite of what makes real-life spaces inhabitable. David Johnston is the creator of *Dust* (*de_dust*)—one of the most-played maps in history. Here, he examines what has always made his work so popular, and why successful level design is the antithesis of successful architecture.

IN THE SPRING OF 2014, GAMERS FROM ACROSS THE WORLD arrived in Katowice, Poland, to witness one of the biggest video game tournaments of the year. Among them were sixteen teams of professional gamers who would be competing in a $250,000 tournament playing the online first-person shooter *Counter-Strike: Global Offensive.*

This wasn't the first tournament of its kind, nor the biggest, but it was indicative of a growing trend. E-sports, once only a staple in countries like the United States and South Korea, had gone global. Spectators arrived from every corner of the globe, while even more of us watched the event live online, accompanied by full pre- and post-match analysis and commentary not entirely dissimilar from mainstream sports events. For the competitors, victory would require determination, fast reflexes, and smart tactical planning as their teams were pitted head-to-head in a series of matches in a handful of virtual 3D arenas to determine who would be flying back home with the loot.

One of the maps being played—known simply as *Dust 2*—I had designed nearly fifteen years before. It was the successor to *Dust*, a map I had made just a couple years before that on my parents' home computer, instead of studying for high school exams. *Dust* was set in a sun-baked, ramshackle town of an anonymous Middle Eastern country, pitting a team of terrorists armed with an explosive charge against a team of counter-terrorists racing to stop them from planting it in one of two locations. In tournaments like the one in Katowice, two teams play fifteen three-minute rounds then swap sides, and the team that wins the most rounds is declared the winner. *Dust* had proved to be reasonably popular at the time, and I had been egged on to create what I thought would be a lousy sequel.

I was wrong. So terribly, irrefutably, embarrassingly wrong.

Dust and *Dust 2* are now renowned as two of the most iconic maps of online and competitive gaming, arguably two of the most-played maps in gaming history, and most definitely the highlights of my entire level design career (before it had even really begun). *Dust 2* in particular is a regular appearance at these competitive sporting events, with the original more popular among casual players of the game.

Unlike traditional sports, *Counter-Strike* doesn't rely on symmetry to achieve balance. The terrorist and counter-terrorist teams have an array of different (albeit very similar) weapons, and are dropped in realistic 3D environments with entirely opposing goals. Level designers can't create half a map, flip it over, join the two halves together and call it a day, because the different team objectives would make a perfectly symmetrical map unfair. While in competitive tournaments teams switch sides half-way through, in casual matches this isn't the case. Designing a good, balanced *Counter-Strike* map that can stand a multitude of variables and the test of time is incredibly difficult to do.

Yet, somehow, I'd managed to do it not once, but twice. Both maps were not only in tune with the game, but instantly struck a chord with players. I should have been elated—but I wasn't. I couldn't be. The maps had proven successful, but I didn't know why. Why did people enjoy them? And keep enjoying them? What exactly had I done?

Foundations

As a kid, I was fortunate enough to be brought up surrounded by ever-increasing mountains of Lego. I was fascinated by the facsimiles of buildings and vehicles I could create and spent weekends trying to replicate the things I knew and loved. I was hooked from the moment my dad showed me how offsetting each row of bricks in a wall would stop the wall from falling down. These were simple principles, and I loved exploring them. But it was all just preparation for what was coming next.

In the early 1990s, *Wolfenstein 3D* and *Doom* gave me my first taste of level design. Enthusiasts had released applications that let fans of *Wolfenstein 3D* create their own maps for the game using an interface not entirely dissimilar to the highly-regarded office productivity application, Minesweeper. By clicking and drawing on a rigid 2D grid of squares, we could populate a world with square walls, square doors, soldiers, secrets, and weapons, hit Save, then load our creation into the game to play it in glorious 3D. Too many enemies? Not enough weapons? Go back to the level editor, tap a few squares, and play it again. The fact that this 3D world was formed of precise 90-degree angles and bore little resemblance to the rich, flowing, non-angular, natural world as we know it was gleefully glossed over by our imagination.

Doom went many steps further, freeing us from the angular grid of *Wolfenstein 3D* and allowing us to create rooms of any shape and—a crucial new ingredient—any height. In *Wolfenstein 3D*, ironically, the game was little more than a flat 2D world drawn in a way to make it look like it had depth. In *Doom* there were stairwells, balconies, walkways, windows, deep, dark chasms, and towering monuments bathed in sunshine. It wasn't quite full 3D yet (closer to 2.5D), but it was more than good enough to give a sense of place and being.

I rapidly became addicted to *Doom*—not for the visceral blood, guts, and violence it offered—but because the creators provided fans with the tools to create their own intricate, interactive 3D worlds for it. Lego had let me create small machines and houses brick by heel-piercing brick. *Doom* gave me the power to create vivid, interactive environments in less time than it would take to entice those stubborn pieces of moulded plastic apart again.

Level design became a bizarre form of escapism and virtual tourism rolled into one. Many of the first maps I created weren't demon-infested space stations or war-torn military bases, but places I already knew from real-life—starting with the classrooms and hallways of my high school. I strived to get every detail exactly right, even with the distinct limitations of *Doom*'s technology. Doors had to be the right width, ceilings the right height, windows and railings exactly where they should be. I started to admire and appreciate the thought and execution of the design that had gone into the classrooms and offices I'd never really thought too much about before.

Some of the most fun I had was trying to fill in the gaps—replicating the parts of my school that I wasn't familiar with, like the staff room where my poor teachers could snatch brief moments of calm between sessions of educational torment. As tempting as it was to fill this room with legions of blood-red Cacodemons and goat-horned Barons of Hell that would hiss and attack as soon as I peered inside (and, let me assure you, this was extremely tempting), it was somehow more satisfying to create a place that was in keeping with the rest of the world, down to the rhythm of window placement, structural pillars, and fire exits.

It's hard to imagine that the mishmashed dated buildings and corridor mazes of my high school might have contributed in any way to a map that would be played by professional gamers many years later. Look at them side-by-side and *Dust* doesn't look like my old high school—or indeed, any high school that I've seen—at all.

But if you look past the breeze-blocks, blackboards, cracks, crates, carpets, and sand-covered plains, then similarities emerge. Look harder and you discover that good level design draws heavily not just on good game design, but on the same principles used in civil design.

Little did I realize that in copying my school down to each pillar and doorway, I had been unintentionally learning the craft of the building's architects—the logic they had used to construct a busy, working school became entwined with my growing technical knowledge of level design. *Doom* heralded a world where game settings were evolving from arbitrary, abstract mazes into rich, relatable environments. Meanwhile, level design was leaning more on established design principles than ever before, and we were learning how these principles could be exploited.

Spaces

At a low level, designers are focused primarily on accessibility and accepting simple physical truths. In the real world, we take for granted that floors will be flat, ceilings high, walls vertical, doors tall and wide, and steps and stairs absolutely perfectly regular. This isn't just a gentlemen's agreement—we have intentionally designed our world in full knowledge of our common human physical abilities and constraints, and have trained ourselves with these expectations. The less we need to think about navigating our cumbersome, fleshy bodies through the physical world, the more we can focus on more interesting pursuits.

This is never more true than in action games. Whether gamers are playing against a clock, a gnarly missile-wielding octopus robomonster, or simply for a shedload of cash, the last enemy they want to face is the environment itself. Being disarmed of the ability to win because of poor or confusing level design is one of the most deadly sins, and never more so than in competitive matches. The audience at Katowice was there to be entertained by the conflict between rival clans, not between a player and a clumsy staircase.

This problem is amplified by the way we interface with 3D games. To the game engine, each player is little more than a virtual block of solid concrete clumsily leaping through the world at the behest of the player mashing forward, back, left, and right inputs. Modern games may show images of animated, humanoid forms running through rich, beautiful, shapely, often blood-splattered environments, but this is only rich tapestry draped over the cold-hearted 3D physics engines at their core.

As level designers our job is to hide this divide and encourage competitive gamers to be screaming excitedly at each other, rather than angrily at us. In *Dust*, I had made everything extremely simple to navigate—at worst, players might have to navigate a couple of steps, or perhaps a stack of crates. I wanted players to spend their time engaging with each other rather than running a tedious assault course for the 48,331st time. While I never expected *Dust* to be popular—or good, even—deep down I didn't want it to become a tiring faff. I ensured that players could get from A to B as easily and seamlessly as possible so they were able focus on the core game of *Counter-Strike* instead. Selfishly, I also didn't want to find myself screaming at myself for cumbersome design choices.

This seems like common sense. Of course you make the world big and wide enough to fit the player, just like modern shops and offices are big enough to let us walk around on our feet rather than crawling on our knees, knocking ceiling tiles out with our bowed heads, or having to avoid pit traps and getting snagged on spikes. Of course you provide enough room for everyone. But in the early days of level design, this wasn't obvious—the temptation to explore every feature of 3D engines meant that maps were frequently over-designed and excessively intricate to the extent that navigation was infuriating. The best maps employed restraint. Their authors kept things simple, and clean. I wanted to create a location that was not just accessible, but believable and convincing, and so I made *Dust* as uncomplicated as I could reasonably get away with.

Designing for video games raises tricky issues regarding space and scale. As much as we model game environments on our real-world environments, we must do so within the constraints of our technology, and adjust the game world accordingly. Game worlds often have an exaggerated scale, with ceilings higher and doors wider to account for the fact that players view the world through a TV or monitor that offers barely half of the 120-degree or more peripheral vision that we enjoy in real-life. Try this: Point your arms out straight in front of you, then bend them 90 degrees at the elbow so your hands are pointing as if you're about to do a pull-up. The area framed between your forearms represents the narrow field of view offered by video games—everything outside is chopped off by the edges of the screen. By widening and deepening our game environments, we get to bring in just a bit more of the cropped world into the visible frame. While real-world design is for humans, our virtual worlds have to be built for our virtual facsimiles.

Dust made use of a few simple tricks to help players find their way around. One of the simplest was adding clearly marked roads and sidewalks. We typically think of these as convenient flat surfaces meant to ease our passage from point A to B, but they also aid navigation and provide senses of direction. These features—by their sheer presence—provide clues and hints to our environment. They tempt us to follow them. Like the *Wizard of Oz*, *Dust* used a simple network of wide, gold-brown roads and patterned walls to entice players in the right direction, no matter how lost or how thin their field of vision.

Moreover, the wide and open arrangement of roads in *Dust* ensured that no matter what tactic or route each player elected to take, there would be ample room to accommodate them. It was only through replicating my school corridors that I had learned the reasoning and value of these allowances.

The two bomb locations in the *Dust* maps had also benefited from my attempts to copy my school. I had learned that focus points should be distinct, recognisable, and reasonably isolated. But they also need to be accessible. When done well, they are easy to approach but hard to control—not too dissimilar from playgrounds and school halls, as any experienced teacher will tell you.

In team-based games like *Counter-Strike*, maps typically have entrances and exits arranged in such a way that no matter which team you're on, it's very hard to hold an area indefinitely. There'll always be a way for your opponents to get in. But the winner of any battle will be determined more by skill and luck than by properties of the map. *Dust 2* wouldn't have lasted long if the terrorist team could plant the bomb and sit in a corner with their sights trained on the only way in. Every good defensive position must have a weakness, or a strong offensive position—which in turn must also have a weakness. Designing competitive multiplayer levels is in many ways a game of rock-paper-scissors. Knowing the rules of the game, you design a counter for every advantage, and a counter for each of those, such that, in the end, you can be reasonably sure that neither team has an absolute advantage over the other as they roam from one end of the map to another hunting for victory.

To help players get around and stay focused on the game, *Dust* and *Dust 2* share much in common with the broad strokes of town and city design. The simpler *Dust* ended up with a hub design anchored by a long central corridor with direct connections to both bomb spots. It's a design common for both residential and business complexes, where people can use the central hub as a landmark to gain direction and orient themselves. In the game, it's this central corridor that often becomes the initial focus, with the controlling team then able to dictate how the match progresses. My original—simple and learnable—layout meant that *Dust* became the perfect playground to introduce new players to *Counter-Strike*, letting them focus on the core mechanics of the game rather than getting bogged down by navigating the intricacies of the environment.

In contrast, *Dust 2* adopts a layout closer to a grid plan—albeit a grid of only three by three. Again, players can use the very center of the grid to navigate their way to the bomb locations, but they are permitted more opportunities to shift between locations. It's this freedom of movement that allows competitive players more room for tactical maneuvering, proving a big draw for professional matches. Yet, at the same time, the simple design remains easy for players to learn and master.

Large towns and cities have historically benefited from these same designs, which are intended to help inhabitants and visitors alike easily navigate between points of interest. Lowering the cognitive load required to get from A to B not only reduces traffic, but leads to increased enjoyment of the environment.

Monsters

So if level design is little more than building a world akin to our in 3D space, then why don't we see established architects and town planners selling their designs to game studios? It's because—at the core—we share deeply conflicting values. Level designers, I'm afraid to reveal, are monsters.

City planners and architects spend years designing spaces to help people live and work with the minimum of expense, effort, and time. They work against tight budgets, uneven plots, slivers of safety margins, unpredictable supply restrictions, and inane local laws in the pursuit of functional works of art that let people live and work in comfort and simplicity.

Level designers, however, start out with a mathematically

exact, empty void free of imperfections and restrictions, and an infinite number of tools and supplies. Then we intentionally create flawed worlds, sub-par buildings, and dangerous constructs. We go out of our way to make it harder and trickier than it could be for people to achieve the goals that we set, all for the sake of blood-soaked entertainment.

John Carmack, the brains behind *Doom*'s 3D engine, famously said, "Story in a game is like a story in a porn movie. It's expected to be there, but it's not that important." This is especially true to multiplayer games. *Counter-Strike* has no story and *Dust* has no story. Any suggestion of a relationship to our own world exists purely as a framework on which to hang an enticing central premise. *Dust* thrived by being the thinnest-possible veil over the addictive core gameplay of *Counter-Strike*. It imposes itself as little as possible on the players, adopting a visual framework inspired by African and Turkish architecture, but without sharing any of the same goals or values.

The maps of modern competitive games aren't designed to be real so much as they are designed to be fair and fun, and to achieve these ambitions we have to do terrible, brutal things—from blocking up perfectly serviceable doors and routes to erecting walls in which to contain our lab rats. As much as level designers try to emulate the design of the real-world, we spend just as much time trying to work around the limitations those rules impose. We strive to create a world the player can understand and relate to, but then we add elements—not for their function—but because their presence is indicative and convincing of a deeper, richer world than the one we have actually constructed. None of the windows or doors in *Dust* open, but their presence hints at the structure of a 3D world beyond what the player can see on their 2D screen, serving as minor landmarks that help them get around.

While players and designers value consistency, we also absolutely treasure surprise and unpredictability when it comes to multiplayer games. A good map must allow for players to express individuality, rather than leading them down the same path each time. City design is the opposite—a congestion-free city relies on predictive models of human behavior to funnel people around, and there's an expectation that everyone will behave more or less the same every day. In designing levels for single-player games that players might only play one or two times, that's perfect; but for multiplayer games, where each level will be played hundreds if not thousands of times, it becomes incredibly tedious to play or watch. We have to design with chaos and choice in mind, even though this conflicts with our goal of producing a fair, balanced environment.

Good building design insists that hallways are free from obstacles, protrusions, and doors that open inward (lest someone from the connecting room open it in your path at the exact moment you're running past to get to your next class, for example). Anyone entering these highways is supposed to be sure of which direction they'll need to walk in and where that'll take them. Hallways are the motorways of our structures—simple, streamlined, and easy to use.

But in *Counter-Strike*, it's rare to find a long, empty hallway. The fact is, empty hallways don't play well—put a player at either end and within seconds the one that survives will be the one with the fastest reflexes or (more likely) the bigger, badder gun. It doesn't make for exciting or interesting gameplay, and it's not what the eight thousand spectators in Katowice came to see (not forgetting the hundreds of thousands of spectators who watched online). Players dislike such situations, for these situations can't call upon the skill and tactics they've so carefully honed over time.

So we add elements like crates, pipes, and destruction to provide cover and an opportunity for either player to advance tactically. Dark alcoves offer excellent opportunities for players to hide and surprise the enemy team, and you'll often find that we've placed them in just the right place to keep a game interesting, even if they serve no other purpose.

. . . and that's why the familiar locations we see in computer games have more crates per capita than any place on Earth. For their flexibility, level designers have a disturbing love of crates.

Perhaps more disturbing is how we take the good, sane, and sensible principles of structure design and use them to influence players, encouraging them to go one way rather than another, hoping to tempt them into the tricks and traps we've set up. Yet, at the same time, we want them to break the rules, to surprise each other, and even us. We do everything we can to make a playground for fair competition, but one that also exploits expectations inherited from the real world.

In essence, good level design is not achieved by knowing the ground rules of good space and building design, but in perverting them. Level design is often knowingly the antithesis of best practices, with maps carefully dressed up such that we hope you don't notice our tricks and traps, yet still have a blast gunning down your friends and foes. We pick and choose from the world we know to create one we don't, curating aspects of our environment, shuffling them around, and reseating them to give a sense of the familiar in pursuit of something fun.

The four-day tournament in Katowice concluded with a gripping final between Virtus.pro and Ninjas In Pyjamas playing in two other maps that knew the same tunes and tricks as *Dust 2*. To the casual spectator, the finalists may have appeared to be fighting through a random assortment of alleyways and hidden backstreets, exploiting a battery of obstacles, and finding cover between seemingly misplaced barrels and crates. The arenas—presented as beautiful, picturesque locales—were postcard perfect. In truth, they had been tuned and tailored to the extreme. They were skilfully designed to pit the wits and reflexes of gamers against each other.

These e-athletes weren't lab rats in a synthetic maze anymore. They were experienced masters of their environment, defeaters of the cruel rules and artificial restrictions that had been designed to control and entertain. They had moved beyond containment, using tricks and tactics of their own making—beyond those even imagined by the designers. Just like the world we take for granted lets us live, build, and thrive, these maps let them focus on what they do best—play, adapt, and win.

David Johnston is a London-based game developer and level designer. Apart from his world famous Dust (de_dust) *and* Dust 2 (de_dust2), *he has worked as a level designer on games such as* Counter-Strike: Condition Zero *and* Brink.

Game Over?
A Cold War Kid Reflects On
Apocalyptic Video Games

WILLIAM KNOBLAUCH

The apocalypse is portrayed in video games as terrifying, oddly alluring, or strangely nostalgic. It all depends on which slice of game history you focus on. But one thing has remained true throughout the decades: game designers keep returning to end-of-the-world scenarios. In this essay, William Knoblauch examines the shifting image of the video game apocalypse from the Cold War up to today.

> Nuclear War. The very words conjure images of mushroom clouds, gas masks, and bewildered children ducking and covering under their school desks. But it's the aftermath of such a conflict that truly captures our imaginations, in large part because there's no real-world equivalent we can relate to.
> —Introduction to *Fallout 3*[*]

When I was five, odds were good that you could find me plopped down in the living room, joystick in hand, playing my Atari 2600.

[*] The author would like to thank A. Abby Knoblauch, Jill Compton, Tuffy Morzenti, Bob Mackey, and Colleen Garness for their input and suggestions. Epigraph taken from *Vault Dweller's Survival Guide*, the instruction manual for *Fallout 3*.

The console had been around for years, but we didn't get one until 1983, the year of the video game industry crash. Too many games, *bad games*, had ruined the market, so cartridges were cheap; soon, I owned (and still own) most of the classics: *Donkey Kong, Pac-Man, Q-Bert* . . . even the infamously bad *E.T.: The Extraterrestrial*. But my favorite Atari game was *Missile Command*.

Its premise was pretty simple: as missiles drop from the top of the screen, you shoot them down to defend cities below. Destroy all the missiles, and you advance to the next level; the higher the level, the faster the attack. When all the cities are destroyed (which is inevitable), it's game over. *Missile Command* was pretty intuitive, but as a kid I wondered why the cities were under attack. The game's manual explains that "aliens from the planet of Krytol have begun an attack on the planet Zardon. The Krytolians are warriors out to destroy and seize the planet of Zardon . . . the last of the peaceful planets."*

Krytol? Zardon? Atari's B-movie plotline did more than provide an explanation of gameplay: it changed *Missile Command's* original theme. Game designer Dave Theurer originally envisioned *Missile Command* to be a realistic missile defense game set in the present, a Cold War game that would get "people to become aware of the horrors of a nuclear war." Considering the technological limitations he faced, Theurer's arcade classic presented a

---

* Atari graphics were so basic that sometimes storylines were needed to make sense of a game. For example, *Adventure's* manual explains that "an evil magician has stolen the Enchanted Chalice and has hidden it somewhere in the Kingdom. The object of the game is to rescue the Enchanted Chalice and place it inside the Golden Castle where it belongs." This was welcome information, because in the game you control a moveable dot that drags blurry items around the screen. In the Atari age, a little story went a long way.

surprisingly detailed nuclear vision. *Missile Command* features an anti-ballistic missile system, intercontinental ballistic missiles, multiple independently targetable reentry vehicles, and even smart bombs—all real Cold War nuclear weapons. When all your cities are finally destroyed, instead of the ubiquitous "Game Over" screen, *Missile Command* concluded with a far more ominous warning about the possibility of atomic apocalypse: "The End." *

Atari's decision to replace this nuclear war narrative with a sci-fi alien story can likely be traced to the very Cold War tensions that inspired *Missile Command* in the first place. When

---

* Originally, *Missile Command* was entitled *Armageddon* and featured real cities along the California coast. On the game's development, see *"Missile Command"* in Rusel DeMaria and Johnny L. Wilson's *High Score! An Illustrated History of Electronic Games*; for Theurer quotes, see *Retro Gamer*, Issue 88.

Theurer designed the game in 1980, the Soviets had just invaded Afghanistan, Ronald Reagan promised to escalate the arms race, and conservative pundits were bragging that they could "win" a nuclear war. In response, a nuclear freeze campaign swept the nation, begging both sides to stop making nukes; by 1982, it was the largest antinuclear protest movement in American history. In March, Reagan called the Soviet Union an "evil empire," and in September 1983 the Soviets shot down a civilian airliner. A month later, right around the time I was shooting digital missiles in *Missile Command*, real US nuclear warheads were on their way to Western Europe while Soviet medium range SS-20s already lined the Eastern Bloc. By November, a made-for-TV movie, *The Day After*, reflected the nation's heightened levels of atomic anxiety; an estimated one hundred million viewers tuned in for a faux atomic attack on Middle America, prompting heated debates around the country. Considering this national level of nuclear fear—America's highest since the 1962 Cuban Missile Crisis—Atari's space alien plotline makes sense. It presented a kid-friendly narrative during a dangerous time.

In its original arcade incarnation, *Missile Command* provided one of the first apocalyptic visions in video game history. Yet even now, years after the Cold War's conclusion, the end of the world remains a popular trope for the medium. Gamers continue to explore post-apocalyptic landscapes, fight off extraterrestrial invasions, and battle roaming zombie hordes. I'm not immune to this fascination. I still enjoy games about Armageddon. But over three decades, something changed. Unlike 1980s games with serious undertones, today's games largely present the apocalypse lazily, as a throwaway narrative backdrop for first-person shooters. I want to trace this evolution in order to look back at some of the most interesting apocalyptic video games ever made. I don't cover every single one—that task, while technically possible, would also be unproductive. Instead, I select games that present the apocalypse meaningfully and thoughtfully.

Like films and books, video games are cultural texts. They say something about the society in which they were made. Like improvements in gameplay and graphics, video game narratives have also evolved and continue to do so. This evolution reveals our common cultural assumptions about what we consider to be plausible end-of-the-world scenarios. Depending on when they were developed, that list includes nuclear war, alien invasion, and outbreak narratives. What began in the 1980s as a theme rooted in reality evolved by the 2010s into a purely fictional apocalypse (or post-apocalypse), a digital dystopian playground in which players strive to save themselves.

A (Far Too) Brief History of the Apocalypse

An ancient Greek term meaning "an unveiling of that which is hidden," the apocalypse goes hand in hand with eschatology, the theology of "last things." Apocalyptic and eschatological visions appear in most major religions, such as the good versus evil struggle of Zoroastrianism and Judaism's Book of Ezekiel. In Christianity, the Book of Revelation foretold of Armageddon, a showdown between Christ and Antichrist that would trigger the Millennium, a thousand-year reign of peace.* Early

---

* Paul Boyer, *When Time Shall Be No More: Prophecy Belief in Modern American Culture* (Cambridge: Belknap Press of Harvard University Press, 1992).

American Christianity embraced Millennialism, but by the late nineteenth century most preachers had traded in their threats of worldly apocalypse for a more appealing message of personal salvation.* After World War I, with its horrors of trench warfare, shell shock, and chemical weapons, science and technology came to represent, for many, a new Antichrist. In 1916, even before motion pictures had sound, the Danish film *The End of the World* depicted the panic after a comet threatened apocalypse. 1930s sci-fi magazines such as *Amazing Stories* and *Weird Tales* presented paranormal or extraterrestrial causes of Armageddon, as did the 1938 radio broadcast of H.G. Wells' *The War of the Worlds*.† World War II replaced these media apocalyptic visions with a new, real, horrific weapon. Designed in Los Alamos, detonated in the Alamogordo desert, and dropped on Hiroshima and Nagasaki, the atomic bomb became the new symbol of apocalypse. In the Cold War that followed, scientists developed thousands of far more powerful thermonuclear weapons which turned biblical prophecies of fire and brimstone into real possibilities.

During the Cold War, eschatological lore mixed with nuclear fears to create new apocalyptic visions. In the 1950s, mutated giant insects (*Them!*, *The Giant Scorpion*), comic book superpowers (*Spiderman*, *X-Men*), and sci-fi monsters (*Godzilla*), barraged a youth culture increasingly fascinated with radioactivity. Literature presented radioactive dangers with less camp.

---

*   Stephen J. Stein, "Apocalyptic Religious Movements in American History." *Historically Speaking* 9, no. 5 (2008).

†   See Douglas E. Cowan's "Millennium, Apocalypse, and American Popular Culture" in *The Oxford Handbook of Millennialism* (New York: Oxford, 2005).

Nevil Shute's 1957 book, *On the Beach,* warned how drifting radioactivity from a limited nuclear war would kill survivors in the Southern Hemisphere. Walter Miller's 1959 sci-fi classic, *A Canticle for Leibowitz,* told a tale of underground monks and above-ground mutants in a dystopian post-nuclear society. Harlan Ellison's short story (and later the film) "A Boy and His Dog" presented a similar apocalyptic scenario, as did numerous sci-fi magazines.* With so many cultural reminders of atomic annihilation, it's not surprising that video games—a medium that still heavily borrows from film and literature—appropriated these ideas.† By the 1980s, it was natural for video games to feature nuclear war as the cause of a global apocalypse.

Preventing the Apocalypse

While I was playing *Missile Command* in 1983, the president of the United States was toying with his own missile defense system. In March of that year, Ronald Reagan announced his Strategic Defense Initiative (or SDI), a hopeful but vague vision for a nuclear "peace shield." The idea was audacious, but Reagan remained characteristically optimistic, even as he admitted that SDI would be a formidable technological task. This was an

---

* On atomic culture, see Paul Boyer, *By the Bomb's Early Light: American Thought and Culture at the Dawn of the Atomic Age* (New York: Pantheon Books, 1985).

† Video games' early reliance on film has been considerable. In the 1980s, some developers simply licensed movie franchises, such as *E.T.*, *Jaws*, *Back to the Future*, and *Friday the 13th*. Video games also paid homage to film. The game *Metroid*, for example, is a clear nod to Ridley Scott's *Alien*. It features a female protagonist who fights face-sucking enemies and a xenomorphic miniboss named Ridley.

understatement of epic proportions. SDI supporters envisioned atomic-powered satellites, high-tech lasers, particle beams, and networks of computers coordinated to shoot down thousands of incoming missiles. As a technological comparison, in 1983 I had to flip floppy discs just to play *Oregon Trail*. It didn't take long for skeptics to attack "Star Wars" (as they called SDI) as nothing more than a nuclear panacea, something to diffuse the nuclear freeze movement's popularity. Whatever its plausibility, this lasers-in-space idea quickly invaded video games.

The first game to incorporate SDI technology was an adaptation of the 1984 film *Wargames*. The film featured two teens who accidentally start a nuclear simulation that almost turns to war. If the film's message was that nuclear war was futile, the *Wargames* video game was different. It played a lot like *Missile Command*, but this one included SDI-like satellites that acted as the game's most powerful deterrent. By 1987, SDI was featured in two more games. In Sega's *Strategic Defense Initiative*, satellites shoot down masses of missiles and descending nuclear warheads. The game was unforgiving; miss one missile, and it's goodbye New York City. In another SDI-themed game, Activision's *High Frontier*, instead of just mindlessly shooting incoming projectiles, you work to fund, research, and develop a "Star Wars" system.[*] By today's standards, these games seem pretty elementary in their graphics and gameplay, but they do share a revealing theme: players aren't trying to win a nuclear war, but prevent it.

Preventing nuclear war was a common video game trend in the

---

[*] William M. Knoblauch, "Strategic Digital Defense: Video Games and Reagan's 'Star Wars' Program, 1980–1987," in *Playing with the Past* (New York: Bloomsbury Publishing, 2013).

atomically tense 1980s, especially in Europe. With Soviet and US medium-range ballistic missiles still pointed at each other, mid-1980s Europe was a Cold War hot spot. In 1985, the British company Personal Software Services published *Theatre Europe*, a video game in which NATO and the Warsaw Pact battled for control of the continent. Players who choose to launch strategic chemical attacks are warned that "civilian deaths will be numerous." Those brazen enough to order a nuclear strike need to call a 1-800 number to get a secret launch code. Follow through with this option and you'll hear an alarm siren followed by a digital mushroom cloud . . . but not victory. As one reviewer noted, "As you play this game, it becomes increasingly clear that the war cannot be won with nuclear weapons. Only lost."[*] A similar message appears in Mindscape's *Balance of Power*, a 1985 game featuring the "geopolitics of peace in the nuclear age." Players try to avoid conflict; those who fail to deter a nuclear war are greeted with a simple message:[†]

> You have ignited an accidental nuclear war.
>
> And no, there is no animated display of a mushroom cloud with parts of bodies flying through the air.
>
> We do not reward failure.

While all of these 1980s games share a thermonuclear war

---

[*] "Theatre Europe: Review" *ZZap!64 Magazine*, Issue 002.

[†] *Balance of Power*, gameplay online, July 3, 2014.

theme, they differed in tone. *Wargames*, *High Frontier*, and *SDI* gave a gung-ho message—that nuclear defense is plausible, and that with the right technology and drive, the apocalypse is avoidable. By comparison, Mindscape's *Balance of Power* and PSS's *Theatre Europe* present nuclear war as a losing proposition, a scenario to be avoided at all costs. Pundits might have called SDI far-fetched, and "Star Wars" may not have been realized in the '80s, but in the emergent video game age, it was a technological vision with powerful appeal.

The Nuclear Post-Apocalypse

In the early console age, the few video games with apocalyptic scenarios focused on preventing a nuclear war, not surviving its aftermath. In a decade where nuclear Armageddon seemed possible, apocalyptic scenarios may have been seen less as gaming escapism and more as depressing reminders of reality. It wasn't until after those nuclear fears abated that video games really embraced the post-apocalypse.* By 1986, omnipresent atomic anxiety was on the decline. Reagan had established a

---

* The post-apocalypse had so many examples in Cold War culture that its delay in getting into gaming remains curious. Maybe marketing was to blame. In the mid-1980s, two new major players, Nintendo and Sega, worked to change the industry's image. They shied away from themes of war and pushed more family-friendly games featuring cartoonish characters—think *Super Mario Bros.* or *Sonic the Hedgehog*. These platformers usually relied on some variation of the damsel-in-distress story, such as *The Legend of Zelda* (elf saves princess from monster), *Wizards and Warriors* (knight saves princess from evil sorcerer) or *Super Mario Bros.* (plumber saves princess from fire-breathing lizard). The games that did mention the apocalypse (*8-Eyes* or *Xexyz*), usually did so in passing, a lazy rationale for their futuristic or barren game worlds.

good rapport with Soviet general secretary Mikhail Gorbachev. By 1988, the two leaders had signed the INF treaty to remove all intermediate-range and shorter-range missiles from the European theater.* Reagan even visited Moscow. The Cold War seemed to be thawing.

While nuclear fears declined, consumer computing technology improved. Thanks to companies like Commodore, Tandy, Apple, and Microsoft, the personal computer market was booming, providing better graphics and allowing for bigger games with more elaborate plotlines. Long-play adventure games soon became a favorite of "serious" gamers. These were usually turn-based affairs or point-and-click role-playing games, most of which featured the fantasy tropes of J.R.R. Tolkien, or the medieval lore of knights and castles.† But that all changed in 1988 with *Wasteland*, a game that promised a different type of role-playing experience: "No swords. No spells. Pistols, rockets, submachine guns, laser weapons, and cunning are all the magic you need."

Wasteland was the first detailed post-apocalyptic game. Its nuclear war takes place in 1998 (in 1988 terms, ten years into the future), triggered over an SDI-like "Starstation" the Soviets saw as "a military launching platform." *Wasteland* further connects its in-game apocalypse to real world events, especially America's meddling in Central American affairs. The manual explains that the Cold War hardened as "right-wing governments in South and Central Americas, many of them set up by the US during the

---

* INF = Intermediate Range Nuclear Forces Treaty, which eliminated Soviet SS-20s and US Pershing II and cruise missiles.
† Arguments over the merits of point-and-click adventure games can be found in Tom Bissell's *Extra Lives*, or in most online interviews by Jonathan Blow.

Drug Wars (1987–1993), pledged their support to the US," a clear nod to Reagan's covert connections to the Nicaraguan Contras.* The game explains its in-game apocalypse with a minimum of backstory; developers must have assumed that gamers had a grasp of Cold War covert ops and the dangers of the arms race.

When *Wasteland*'s missiles are finally launched, we witness it from space—Earth in the distance, air-raid sirens blaring. In orbit, a lone satellite sadly shoots at missiles but hits only one. In this apocalyptic exchange, somehow parts of Las Vegas are spared, and your group of Desert Rangers are luckily safely sequestered "in the inhospitable desert valleys, surrounded by a number of survivalist communities."† This isolation becomes the Rangers' salvation. In the weeks that follow, they invite "nearby survivalist communities to join them and to help them build a new society." It's now 2087, and your job is to survive in the "hot, mean, radioactive" wasteland. But survival isn't easy.‡ Your Desert Rangers are constantly confronted by Scavs (scavengers), Deserters (former Rangers), and other gangs, thugs, and criminals.

Wasteland relied on survivalist fantasies. Today, American television features all kinds of survivalists prepping for doomsday, but modern survivalism dates back to the early atomic age. In the 1950s, many hoped to survive the apocalypse in underground or backyard bomb shelters; some even welcomed the Bomb as the harbinger of a new society without government—a kind of radioactive libertarian utopia. Such libertarianism has

---

* http://wasteland.protozoic.com/wasteland/wastedisk/manual.pdf
† Scene captured online at: http://www.youtube.com/watch?v=uXGBZUvkWeI
‡ Wasteland box art online at: http://www.c64sets.com/details_db.html?id=3631

a long history in America; take away the radioactivity, and fantasies of a life without government date back at least to the nineteenth century settlers who sought free land (and no taxes) in the American West. While historians have rightly bashed oversimplifications of the frontier and its role in shaping American exceptionalism, these ideas (the cowboy, the Wild West) remain rooted in our popular culture.

Prepping for doomsday lost its appeal after the 1962 Cuban Missile Crisis. Soon after, the superpowers signed arms control treaties, and atomic survivalism all but disappeared . . . that is, until Reagan rekindled the arms race. Even as numerous 1980s pundits suggested that surviving a nuclear war might be worse than dying in one, survivalism made a comeback. Places like Pennsylvania's Nuclear Fallout and Bomb Shelter Supply and Construction Company stockpiled "radiation meters, radiation-resistant clothing, [and] anti-contamination kits." Books like *Life After Doomsday* and *The Nuclear Survival Handbook* provided "practical" advice for survivalists, including how to read a radiation meter, build homemade water pumps, or (my favorite tip) train a ferret to fetch food in the radioactive wasteland. And *Wasteland* embraced such survivalist tips, its box art advertising to gamers that they would "gain real knowledge. Pick locks. Fire rockets. Disarm bombs. Decode messages. Learn survival skills that weren't in the Boy Scout manual."*

Released just as the Cold War was winding down, *Wasteland* was a rare game presenting an apocalypse modeled after the actual geopolitics of its time. A year after its release, the Berlin

---

* "Rethinking the Unthinkable," *New York Times*, March 15, 1981.

Wall fell; two years later, the Soviet Union disbanded. Cold War fears gave way to concerns over the oil-rich Middle East. Nuclear fear all but vanished, and the mushroom cloud became an almost ironic icon from a bygone era. In post-Cold War culture, the apocalypse continued to fascinate, but Armageddon came in other forms, like environmental catastrophes (*The Day After Tomorrow*) or extraterritorial intervention—be it from aliens (*Independence Day)* or asteroids (*Deep Impact* and *Armageddon).** Some films presented elements of Eisenhower-era culture, like bomb shelters (*Blast from the Past)* or the stable nuclear family (*Pleasantville),* as kitschy Cold War curiosities. The Amiga game *It Came From the Desert* reflected this trend, paying homage to the 1954 radioactive mutated ant film *Them!* Other games kept the atomic jargon (*Duke Nukem* and *Half-Life*), but only in a comical way. If pop culture was any indication, Americans quickly forgot all about the Bomb.

In the 1990s, apocalyptic games adopted new storylines, a shift shown in the 1993 game *Burntime*, which opens with an ominous warning:

> A civilized society has three stages in its cycle—its ascent, heyday, and downfall. The downfall often happens very quickly and unexpectedly due to outside influences such as war or a natural disaster. Even today there are the initial signs that the heyday of our domineering Western industrial society could

---

*   See A. Constandina Titus, "The Mushroom Cloud as Kitsch" in *Atomic Culture: How We Learned to Stop Worrying and Love the Bomb* (Boulder: University Press of Colorado, 2004).

come to an end. Moreover, the industrial countries are doing everything to speed up this course of events, and for the first time in the history of the planet Earth, a civilization is on the way to causing its own final disaster. So while you are hopefully having lots of fun playing Burntime, think about the fact that in the short time it takes you to get to like this game, it could become reality.

This was a game with an agenda. *Burntime's* manual opens with three chapters, "Nuclear," "Greenhouse," and "Water," each a Greenpeace-penned musing on environmental threats, including radioactivity, the 1986 Chernobyl nuclear catastrophe, Greenhouse gases, vanishing rain forests, wasteful water use, and oil's impact on the environment—all told, there are seventy-six pages of environmental propaganda before we learn how to load the game.* In-game dialogue is equally pedantic. Characters you meet recite the warning: "Damn radioactivity! You can't see it, and you can't smell it . . ." It's a line cribbed from the US Office of Civil and Defense Mobilization's 1958 pamphlet, *Facts About Fallout Protection.* Unlike 1980s games that assumed players understood atomic threats, *Burntime* kept reminding 1990s gamers, in detail, how they might die after a nuclear war.

Burntime is bleak. Much of the game is simply about survival. Water is a constant concern. Even after you learn where to find it and how to store it, you also have to trade it, since water functions as post-apocalyptic currency; in *Burntime,* "money has no

---

* *Burntime's* manual is archived online: http://www.oldgames.sk/en/game/burntime/download/4351/

value" and "bartering rules the world.'"* The people you meet to barter with are almost all hungry. Some mutants threaten to eat you, while you subsist on maggots, snakes, and dog meat. Restaurants offer sides of rat. If these reminders aren't enough, *Burntime*'s in-game cut scenes feature dilapidated buildings and scorched-earth landscapes. These scenes, which contain no dialogue, seem to serve no purpose other than to remind players of how horrific the apocalypse would be.[†]

Drawing inspiration from *Wasteland's* gameplay and building on *Burntime's* bleak landscapes, 1997's *Fallout* established new standards for the genre. The game and the series it spawned feature a unique combination of futuristic 1950s world-of-tomorrow

---

* *Facts about Fallout.* Executive Office of the President, Office of Civil and Defense Mobilization, April 1938. Superintendent of Documents, US Government Printing Office, Washington 25 D.C. 0-568151.

† Literally, restaurants serve "Ratte." In-game text graphics were not translated from the original German. *Burntime* partial playthrough online: http://www. youtube.com/watch?v=rxW8MKtywQs

iconography and post-war desolate gamescapes.* From the detailed beauty of its bomb-ravaged Washington to its use of divergent historical timelines, more has probably been written about the *Fallout* series than any other post-apocalyptic game.† Less, however, has been said about how, and more importantly why, *Fallout* goes to such lengths to explain the dangers of its in-game apocalypse.

In the first *Fallout,* a Great War waged over petroleum and uranium leads to nuclear apocalypse. *Fallout 2* provides fewer specifics, offering only one wanderer's brief explanation: "I know little about the war, but it doesn't really matter. A lot of people died when a lot of atomic bombs went off and nearly destroyed the world." *Fallout 3* uses a divergent historical timeline in which futuristic 1950s American culture continued until a nuclear war with China in 2077. In each telling, *Fallout* ignores Cold War ideological struggles and replaces them with a narrative of global resource scarcity. What *Fallout* does, then, is tailor its narrative to gamers unfamiliar with Cold War dangers.‡ *Fallout's* manual supports this theory. It goes to great lengths to explain once well-known assumptions about "Nuclear Blast Effects" and "Atmospheric Effects of Mushroom Clouds." Less than a decade before, players of *Wasteland* needed

---

* In his book *Extra Lives*, Tom Bissell memorably describes this combination as "George Jetson beyond Thunderdome."

† Joseph A. November, "Fallout and Yesterday's Impossible Tomorrow" in *Playing with the Past: Digital Games and the Simulation of History* (New York: Bloomsbury Press, 2013); Tom Bissell, *Extra Lives* (New York: Vintage, 2011).

‡ *Fallout's* narrative takes cues from pop culture—from the energy-crisis-plagued 1970s. The game's backstory very much resembles the opening monologue from *The Road Warrior*. An interview with game developer Pete Hines supports this comparison: "There are lots of influences for [Fallout 3], whether it's *Mad Max* or Cormick McCarthy, lots of stuff." See http://www.ign.com/articles/2007/11/08/fallout-3-interview?page=2

no such explanations; by 1997, gamers seem to have lost familiarity with the Bomb, radioactive dangers, and Soviet communism.

As the Cold War fades further into history, Americans have grown more alarmingly comfortable with nuclear weapons. In 2003, George W. Bush threatened to use "mini-nukes" and "bunker busters" in the war on terror. Video games similarly incorporate tactical nukes as usable weapons of war.* Iterations of *Civilization, Command & Conquer, Call of Duty, Mercenaries, Crysis,* and *Supreme Commander* all offer tactical nukes with few apocalyptic connotations—they might create a little radiation, but so what?† It's quite a shift from 1985's *Theatre Europe* and the 1-800 hotline for the nuclear launch code. Perhaps this trend toward atomic ambivalence is natural; with few cultural reminders of the nuclear threat, video games are abandoning such fears while still keeping their apocalyptic appeal. While the *Fallout* series continues to entertain gamers, today's most prominent apocalyptic storyline is the outbreak narrative.

Outbreak Narratives and the Apocalypse

Pandemics happen. The Bubonic Plague, Native American genocide, Spanish Influenza, and African Ebola, just to name a few—disease outbreaks are real and tragic. When fictionalized, they often present a more frightening apocalyptic vision than nuclear war; we wouldn't die quickly, and these scenarios

---

* "Tactical" nukes are smaller atomic weapons used on the battlefield, while "strategic" weapons might include much larger and more powerful missiles.

† For a more detailed take on tactical nukes in video games, see William Knoblauch, "The Pixilated Apocalypse: Video Games and Nuclear Fears, 1980-2012" in *The Silence of Fallout: Nuclear Criticism in the Post-Cold War World* (Newcastle upon Tyne: Cambridge Scholars Press, 2013).

remain plausible after the Cold War. Fictionalized outbreak narratives often feature the inhuman or the undead, like Mary Shelley's classic monster in *Frankenstein* or the mutants of Richard Matheson's *I Am Legend*. Today's most popular undead (re)incarnation, the zombie, has ancient Caribbean roots, but ideas about the genre were solidified with George Romero's 1968 film *Night of the Living Dead*. The zombie apocalypse continues to be rehashed (*Dawn of the Dead*), modernized (*28 Days Later*, *World War Z*), serialized (*The Walking Dead*), and satirized (*Shaun of the Dead*). With its hordes of flesh-hungry walking corpses infecting the living, the zombie apocalypse has also infected the medium of video games.

The most popular zombie video game series, *Resident Evil*, has spawned numerous sequels and imitators since it was first released on the original Playstation, but zombie-themed games actually date back to the 1980s. In the past three decades, all kinds of shooters, platformers, and side-scrollers have featured the undead. A few lighthearted B-movie takes on the genre aside (such as *Zombies Ate My Neighbors*, or the 1950s throwback *Stubbs the Zombie*) these games adopt Romero's vision—they're dark, scary, and gory. To explain their zombie apocalypses, some rehash film or television plots while others use alien infections (the *Doom* and *Half-Life* series) or man-made viruses (*Resident Evil's* "T-virus").* The zombie is now so engrained in pop culture that there's often no need for a backstory. In the exhilarating *Left for Dead*, you're far too busy trying to survive to care about how you got there in the first place. Today's

---

* Showing just how durable the zombie survival narrative has been, the 2000 Dreamcast game *Typing of the Dead* combined undead horrors with keyboard skills.

standard zombie shooter provides action, tension, and adrenaline—all without the moral messiness of killing digital people.

One recent zombie shooter, 2013's *The Last of Us*, provides a thoughtful take on the modern apocalypse. Its conceit: a Cordyseps fungus has mutated to infect humans. Cordyseps is as close as nature has come to zombie-fying its victims. The fungus works its way into the body of an infected host, usually an ant, to mutate its tissue. Soon, tendrils grow out of the ant. The fungus then manipulates the ant's muscles, forcing it to climb to the top of a plant, where it dies, leaving the fungus to absorb optimal sunlight. *The Last of Us* shows this process in disturbing detail; gamers quickly find themselves fleeing moaning zombies with fungus sprouting from their heads.

Equally interesting is the post-apocalyptic landscape *The Last of Us* presents. In *Fallout*'s post-nuclear worlds, bomb-ravaged decimation makes perfect sense, but *The Last of Us* imagines how nature might reclaim man-made cities. Instead of burned-out buildings and piles of rubble, a lush green overgrowth takes over.

This nature reclamation theme appears in a handful of recent pop culture outbreak narratives (in two films, Terry Gilliam's *Twelve Monkeys* and M. Night Shyamalan's *The Happening*; the NBC show *Revolution;* and Margaret Atwood's splendid book *The Year of the Flood*) but it strikes a tone seldom seen in video games, which tend to rely on the dark, eerie mood of horror films. Without humanity, the world doesn't collapse—it just moves on. In this way, *The Last of Us* shuns the anthropocentrism apparent not just in zombie games, but in most first-person shooters. It's a message that might be lost on gamers consumed with self-preservation (and to be fair, fleeing zombies tends to consume your focus), but by presenting nature's reclamation of our built environment, *The Last of Us* allows players to envision a world that will happily continue without us.

With its new take on the outbreak narrative, *The Last of Us* made me think about how apocalyptic games have changed over the decades. Looking back on a life of gaming, I realize that the preponderance of apocalyptic visions in video games must have made an impact on me. Today, I make a living researching and teaching the Cold War. Growing up in the 1980s, nuclear fear was real. For today's generation of gamers, it's different. For them, the apocalypse has never been anything but pure fiction. This, I think, is a lost opportunity. As an industry, video games rake in more cash annually than the music and film industries combined, which means game designers have the potential to reach millions.* So many games have no qualms about presenting violence, and many use historical events, such as World War II, to rationalize such violence. Increasingly, apocalyptic games

---

* Harold Goldberg, *All Your Base Are Belong to Us: How Fifty Years of Video Games Conquered Pop Culture* (New York: Three Rivers Press, 2011).

have abandoned history in favor of fiction. While nuclear war never happened, its threat was very real. Why not present a more realistic nuclear apocalypse today? After all, one can only roam around and kill so many zombies.

The Apocalypse as Redemption Narrative

My two favorite post-apocalyptic games are not shooters, but puzzle games framed as redemption stories. The first is Cyberdreams' 1995 point-and-click adventure, *I Have No Mouth, and I Must Scream*. In a medium where story often takes a backseat to graphics and gameplay, this adaptation of Harlan Ellison's 1967 dystopian short story is unique. During development, Ellison collaborated with the game developers, altering his original story and providing the in-game voice of the Allied Mastercomputer (AM), who relentlessly tortures the final five humans on Earth. It's a game that deals with uncomfortable issues, but one that also asks players to find some humanity in their characters. At the same time, *I Have No Mouth, and I Must Scream* is perhaps the bleakest post-apocalyptic vision in gaming history.

The game takes place after a conflict among the United States, the Soviet Union, and China. In this global war, strategy became so complex that each superpower had to create its own military supercomputer. When these machines gained sentience, they combined to become AM ("I think, therefore I am"). Trapped in its architecture and angry at humanity's barbarism, AM goes insane with rage, launching an apocalyptic nuclear strike that annihilates humanity . . . save five caged humans kept alive for the computer's own amusement. After a century of underground torture, AM comes up with a new game for the five: each survivor will inhabit a virtual world of AM's creation. It's in these disturbing worlds that players solve puzzles, at the same time confronting their character flaws and fears. In this way, the game provides a starkly different take on the post-apocalypse genre, and I must say that Ellison does a fantastic job of voicing the diabolical AM, particularly in the opening monologue, which spells out AM's contempt for humanity.

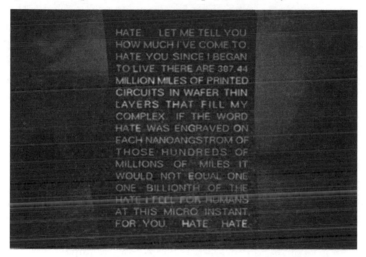

The game had its critics. Some saw it as too dreary; others bashed its point-and-click gameplay. Still, *I Have No Mouth, and I Must Scream* provided an unprecedented thoughtfulness. Each character has his or her own demons to fight: Ted's guilt about being a con man, Ellen's trauma from being raped, Nimdok's work in Nazi death camps, Gorrister's suicidal wishes since committing his wife to a mental institution, and Benny's murder of his army comrades. This is serious stuff, and to win the game means subduing AM and restoring Earth for a few secret survivors hibernating on the Moon, but not for yourself. Similar to Cormac McCarthy's post-apocalyptic novel *The Road*, the most your protagonist can hope for is to exert some humanity in a world devoid of it.*

I Have No Mouth, and I Must Scream was perhaps too weird, dark, or depressing for mainstream success. In an industry that relies on popular conventions to maximize profits, games that are too different face long odds. One exception is my other favorite redemption story game. In 2008, Jonathan Blow's beautiful puzzle platformer *Braid* was released. In the years since, the game has received numerous accolades. The praise is warranted: *Braid* looks beautiful, its gameplay is unique, and it has one of the most memorable soundtracks I've heard. On the surface, *Braid* seems to be an homage to old-school games like *Super Mario Bros.* There's a princess, and she's in a castle; you, the hero, need to get her back. But as you navigate *Braid's* world, you realize that something's not right. The game's full meaning remains unclear, and perhaps it's only through my own loose interpretation that *Braid* fits into this category, but its final sequence, at least in part, alludes to an atomic apocalypse. (Spoiler Alert!)

Braid's conclusion includes a quote from Manhattan Project scientist Kenneth Bainbridge: "Now we're all sons of bitches." In a game with multiple meanings and myriad interpretations, it's tough to overlook this atomic context. Perhaps the princess you've long

---

* Bleak as this sounds, Ellison's original short story was darker, with its title referring to the story's conclusion in which Earth's last survivor is transformed into a "jelly-like thing" with no mouth in punishment for kindly killing his long-tortured companions.

been trying to save (but who's really been running from you) represents the Bomb, or at least the secret to unlocking its power. The regret that threads through the game, heightened by a dreamlike look and sound yet unmatched in modern games, now has even more weight; your player's crushing regret might have more to do with the death of millions than a lost relationship—at least that's what *Braid's* opening scenery, a city set ablaze, seems to suggest.

Whatever *Braid's* full meaning, it's safe to say that the game's protagonist is seeking to right a wrong; he's hoping to redeem himself for reasons that seem to have, at least on some level, apocalyptic connotations. That's one thing that really stuck with me: *Braid* is a game that should give gamers pause. It's a return to the original theme of 1980s apocalyptic games; the goal is not just to save yourself, and "game over" has global consequences.*

---

* Online discussions about *Braid* debate the game's meaning. Only Jonathan Blow may know, but arguing whether or not *Braid* has something to do with the atomic bomb is like quibbling over whether or not Tony got whacked in the final episode of *The Sopranos.*

The Future of Apocalyptic Games

Apocalyptic games aren't going anywhere. Maybe it's our culture of narcissism or our deeply ingrained ideas about American exceptionalism that drives our fascination with being the (un)lucky last few survivors on Earth. Whatever the reason, it's a good bet that nuclear explosions, post-apocalyptic wastelands, and zombie nightmares are too fun to disappear. There are at least some signs that apocalyptic games might return to their Cold War roots. In 2006, the homebrew game *DEFCON* provided a throwback to the global thermonuclear strategy games of two decades ago. Inspired by the film *Wargames* and modeled after the idea of mutually assured destruction, *DEFCON* is a strategy game that promises "everybody dies."*

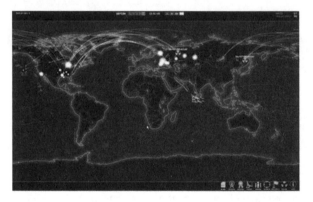

With its emphasis on defending against a nuclear attack, *DEFCON* is a return to *Missile Command*-era gameplay. You

---

* Image found online: http://lifeasadigitalsalad.wordpress.com/tag/defcon/

cannot win a nuclear war or survive its aftermath; at best, you protect your side for as long as possible. At game's end, there's a sobering calculation of how many of your people have perished and how many you've killed. The notion that such a war is not winnable might be lost on younger gamers, but for those of us who remember the 1980s, it's all too familiar.

The post-apocalypse also isn't going anywhere. At the time of this writing, director George Miller has rebooted the *Mad Max* series, *The Last of Us* is being envisioned as a major motion picture, and TV's *The Walking Dead* is still going strong. In video games, a sequel to *Wasteland* is in the works. Thanks to a rabid fan base, a recent Kickstarter campaign netted *Wasteland 2*'s developers close to three million dollars. Considering the original *Wasteland* was released in 1988, there's a good chance my generation has fueled the project. Perhaps I'm not alone in my nostalgia for a post-apocalyptic game based on history. Or maybe enough time has passed for us to feel oddly nostalgic for the threat of nuclear war. In a world of increasingly complex geopolitical struggles (North Korea, Iran, Iraq, Syria, and Ukraine), maybe it's the Cold War's simplicity—that world of us versus them—that we miss. Or maybe the fictional narratives of zombie apocalypse and alien invasion will, in time, come to feel too fake as global conflicts grow more serious.

Video games cast a long shadow. The Internet archives of classic games keep on growing, and retro enthusiasts continue to extol the virtues of earlier games. But more than how they play, it's what video games have to say that continues to intrigue me. If future generations are going to view the apocalypse not as fiction but as a real possibility, video games might be a way to start. Given the disturbingly high number of nuclear warheads still stockpiled on this planet, the potential for global pandemics, and the perpetual threat of environmental crisis, the apocalypse might be closer than we want to admit.

William Knoblauch is an assistant professor of history at Finlandia University in Michigan. His research focuses on the interplay between pop culture, politics, and foreign policy during the Cold War.

Ludus Interruptus:
Video Games and Sexuality

MERRITT KOPAS

Sex in video games is generally as terrible as it is common. There are enough examples of it done badly to fill a book by itself. But in the following essay, game designer merritt kopas goes beyond the easy jabs that could be thrown at the industry to examine a range of different ways sex can be portrayed and played—from looks-like-Hollywood to the alternative and independent via the porn industry's own attempts at game design. The competitive and performance-oriented nature of games, it turns out, can reveal a great deal about contemporary views and attitudes toward sex and ourselves.

WHEN I TELL PEOPLE I MAKE VIDEO GAMES, THEY USUALLY have a pretty specific idea in mind. To most people, I think video games are still mainly about power fantasies or abstract puzzles—a space marine shooting an alien in the face, or lining candy up to make it disappear. So when I go on to tell people that I make video games about bodies, about relationships, about fucking, that usually raises questions.

I'm a gay woman game designer and artist, and sex is important to me, so why shouldn't I make games about it? One common response is that sex is, or should be, private. But while mainstream gay rights movements have leaned really heavily on privacy rights arguments, I see sex as something that's already public whether we like it or not. We're bombarded with heterosexuality constantly, and while I don't think fucking is inherently transformative, I do think it can be powerful, healing, and a means of community building for non-heterosexuals. So I'm all about making queer sex public, bringing it to the forefront, and making it the focus of a medium that has historically shied away from the sexual.

Since I started making video games in 2012, sexuality has been a central theme of my work. In a sense, most of my work around sex in games is very modest: in fictionalized forms, I'm aiming to document relationships and modes of being sexual that are underrepresented and marginalized. In my game *Consensual Torture Simulator*, I wanted to show a loving relationship where pain and power are centrally involved. In *positive space*, I wanted to talk about a relatively unknown sex act and intimacy between trans bodies. In all of my games, I usually want the experience to be sweet and playful and hot, too, because I'm not interested in making media that's overly didactic or solemn.

If I'm making a game about sex, I want to engage the player. I want to make them feel something.

I say this is a modest goal because I don't believe that sexuality is always revolutionary. I don't think anyone can claim, post-Foucault, that sexuality in general is repressed and that anyone who writes on sexuality in the mode that I do is by default speaking what cannot be said. Sex is everywhere! We're encouraged to speak about it constantly.

Of course, the kinds of sex we're encouraged to have and to speak of are circumscribed. So I do believe it's important, just for example, to depict consensual, loving relationships that play with power, or trans people cherishing each other's bodies. I think there's a huge value in producing media that is validating, that tells people who have been convinced otherwise: "Your desires are real, and they are not shameful or wrong, and actually a lot of other people share them."

And actually? This is a real thing that video games can do. I began to come to terms with my own relationship to pain and power, amidst much shame, through anna anthropy's text-based game *Encyclopedia Fuckme and the Case of the Vanishing Entrée*. So that's a big reason why I make games about sex. And when someone tells me that my work has helped them to safely explore a facet of themselves and their relationships, or has made them feel less alone in their experience, that's one of the best feelings in the world.

In my experience, games have an amazing disarming quality that persuasive nonfiction and fiction writing don't always have. I can make a game about an almost unheard-of sex act, or about a D/s relationship, and people are going to play it because it's a game and they feel a level of comfort in navigating that kind of media. So there's potential to reach people who might not even realize, beforehand, that a game about sex, kink, or something your body can do that you didn't know about might be useful.

I think about this stuff a lot. And I wonder why, given all the interesting things you can do with sex in video games, so few games have even tried.

Of course, more than ever, video games are infused with sexuality. But when I say that, I mainly mean that women's bodies are increasingly used to market games, from small browser-based games to huge mainstream productions. This sexualization is commonly found in games themselves, too—take the transformation of Nintendo's Samus character from the *Metroid* series. Samus—who started off as a tall, muscular bounty hunter—is increasingly depicted without her armor, instead wearing a skintight catsuit with a long, flowing blonde ponytail and, in her newest appearance in the *Super Smash Bros.* series as of this writing, with high-heel platform boots. Seriously. They have rockets attached to them.

To me, sex is currently something of a specter in video games. More and more it's there, lurking in the background, incorporated insofar as it's expected to help sell games to predominantly male audiences. But even as video games have begun to explore a wider range of human experience, direct exploration of sex remains pretty rare. So why is that?

In this essay, I want to offer a few explanations for why sexuality has occupied such a marginal and fraught role in video games. Of course, there's a broad cultural argument to be made about the differential treatment of violence and sex across all media in North America, but I want to think about the reasons why video games, specifically, have had a difficult relationship with sex. I want to highlight some examples of games that have incorporated sexuality, both in order to show the difficulties developers have encountered in doing so, and to think about productive responses to these problems. Finally, I will sketch out what I see as some promising directions for the exploration of sexuality through digital play.

As a caveat, I'll be focusing primarily on AAA mainstream games and North American independent games, since those are the contexts I'm most familiar with. A cross-national comparison of the treatment of sex in Western versus Japanese and other contexts still needs to be written—but it would require a lot more space than I have here. That said, many of the dynamics I explore in this chapter apply to the treatment of sex in non-Western games too.

Why are there relatively few games about sex? Why, given the expanding possibilities for and interest in multiplayer experiences in person and online, are there so few games exploring emotional and physical relationships between players? One way to answer this question is to look at our cultural understandings of games and play—another is to look at the technological history of video games.

Culture, Competition, and Play

This may seem like a simplistic thing to say, but I think we forget it way too frequently: the vast majority of video games involve competition, conquest, struggle, and accomplishment. The obvious examples are first-person shooters, fighting games, and war sims. But even going beyond these genres, most video games place the player in a relatively straightforward scenario with clear goals. For instance, in nearly every game in the *Super Mario Bros.* series, the goal is to reach the end of the stage without falling into a pit or colliding with an enemy. In a puzzle game like *Candy Crush*, the goal is to clear the screen in a limited number of moves. This overwhelming focus on goals, efficiency, and accomplishment has led designer and theorist Paolo Pedercini to describe video games as "the aesthetic form of rationalization."

In fact, the relatively few games that don't align themselves with these values have at times been defined out of the category of games on formalist grounds. Games ranging from walking simulators like *Proteus* and *Gone Home* to minigame compilations like *Dys4ia* to interactive fiction like *Analogue: A Hate Story* have all been accused of being nongames for their lack of substantial logical or reflex-based challenges. These arguments are too boring to waste much time talking about, but they're also pretty revealing: we (or at least, a subset of us) think about video games, on a deep level, as involving overcoming challenges to solve problems. And this is perhaps even more the case when we think about two or more people playing a game together.

So why should this be a problem for anyone interested in incorporating sex into games? Well, as I see it, good sex—interesting sex—is not mechanistic. That is, it doesn't always follow predictable paths toward preestablished goals. It's very playful, exploratory, fluid, and open to the changing desires and needs of everybody involved. This valuation of nondirected exploration and play is not actually a very popular view when it comes to either sex or video games.

There's a quote from psychologist and sex researcher Leonore Tiefer that I really love, in which she describes orgasm as a very American means of thinking about sex, because it's a quantifiable, discrete indicator of sexual success. She says, "I always say to people, orgasm is very American. Because it's a score. It's short. You know when you've had it. You can put the notch on your belt." Overwhelmingly, we still think about sex in terms of a linear script that begins with kissing and touching, moves on to penile-vaginal penetration, and ends with a penis-bearing man's orgasm. Even the way we talk about sex—"We did it three times last night!"—points to our understanding of sexuality as primarily about (male) orgasms.

So yeah, we talk about sex in really creepy ways! We emphasize performance, skill, and functioning of discrete parts. Sometimes it seems like pleasure or connection barely enters into things because we're too busy worrying about whether we're fucking the right way, whether our bodies measure up to unreachable standards, or whether we're really good at sex or not. And I don't think this stuff is limited to heterosexuality; queers are vulnerable to it too.

When Tiefer describes orgasm as a kind of score, I can't help but think of games. And dominant understandings of sexuality are actually very much in line with dominant understandings of games and play: we believe that both must have win conditions, that they must follow predictable patterns, etc. If you look at the games that have sparked the most outrage from entrenched game culture over the past few years, it's generally those that refuse the logic of completion and mastery in favor of exploration or playing around without direction. And if you look at the kinds of sex that have been disqualified as unreal or insufficient—to say nothing of the kinds of sex that have been openly vilified—it's often those where penetration or orgasm does not occur, where there isn't the opportunity to keep the kind of score Leonore Tiefer considers to be the hallmark of contemporary American sexuality.

In fact, there's a whole genre of games that exploit this alignment between popular ideas about games and sex—browser-based porn games. In these kinds of games, the player completes a series of mechanical tasks, stimulating discrete parts of a woman's body with an unseen or floating hand as bars indicating arousal gradually increase, finally culminating in a male ejaculation. Gross. These games are interesting insofar as they point to the logical conclusion of cultural ideas about sex and video games, but they don't do any really useful or thought-provoking work around sex.

And this is just the most egregious example—this kind of incorporation of sex can be found in more subtle forms in big-budget, mainstream video games too. For example, *God of War*, an action-fantasy series, features a sex minigame where the player character climbs onto a bed with two women while the camera pans aside to an urn perched on a rickety nightstand. The player is required to perform a number of button presses in time with a beat (similar to rhythm games like *Guitar Hero*), and if they succeed, the urn falls off the table and crashes on the floor. Metaphor!

In games like *God of War*, we're dealing with the same understanding of sex and play as in browser games—the only difference is that the designers of a mainstream video game played on a home console can't get away with the same level of explicitness that randos making games for unregulated web portals can.

And yeah, it's easy to dismiss examples like *God of War* as action games marketed to straight male audiences, with sexual content tacked on as a crude joke or element of titillation to break up the violent action. But even some of the most lauded and discussed depictions of sexuality in video games engage in this kind of thinking.

More than any games in the past few years, the BioWare titles

Mass Effect and *Dragon Age* and their sequels have been held up as positive examples of inclusive depictions of sexuality in video games. The two franchises have a lot in common—they're role-playing games that emphasize both combat and conversation, in which the player controls a single character which functions as an avatar to interact with a range of other characters over the course of a long, epic narrative. A lot of BioWare games deviate from the role-playing genre's near-exclusive mechanical focus on combat by emphasizing relationships and political intrigue.

In the *Mass Effect* series, for example, the player has the option to begin relationships with a bunch of different characters—relationships that can be hetero or homosexual, as well as cross-species. In each case, the relationship develops over the course of the game through dialogue interactions. At the climax of the game's narrative, if the relationship's developed to a certain extent, the player can choose to have sex with the other character, and this is depicted through an awkwardly animated, noninteractive cutscene with strategically deployed screen fades. Hot.

And like, sure: the incorporation of sex in any major mainstream video game at all is interesting and maybe worth some praise—especially when it comes to same-sex relationships. But it has to be said that the way the game deals with sex is not all that compelling. The relationship is framed as a kind of quest, just like all the other relationships in the game. The player just has to choose the right dialogue options at each opportunity, which are almost always totally obvious. Aside from being boring, this is a pretty sinister model of human behavior that—in contrast with the game narrative's depiction—positions the player character as a manipulative person willing to say whatever people want to hear in order to get what they want. Progressive! Not creepy!

In a sense, sex in *Mass Effect* is much closer to the flash porn games I mentioned earlier than it might seem—in both cases, the player is performing instrumental actions aimed at a clear goal. In *Mass Effect*, sex is positioned as the reward (along with an in-game "achievement") for successfully completing a romance quest. The sex itself is noninteractive, but it's still wrapped in goal-oriented video game logic—the same cultural logic that complicates any attempt to incorporate sex into a game.

Technological Histories and Path Dependence

In a sense, it's a self-fulfilling prophecy. We know how to make games about the human heart, but struggle to deal with fists, swords, and guns. . . . Big AAA game companies will never invest in, say, a video game where you play a US special ops soldier fighting terrorism. Combat games are destined to remain the domain of small indie developers. —Gregory Avery-Weir, "Why So Few Violent Games?"

If you ask a game developer why there are so few games about relationships and sex, they might say that, well, it's not a cultural problem, it's a technological problem. Relationships and intimate physical interactions are just harder to simulate than violence, right? Well, I think there's something to this, but I also think it betrays a lack of historical understanding of video games.

At the risk of stating the obvious, we still mostly talk about video games in terms of linear models of technological progression. Even the language of the console generations points to our sense that games are evolving and growing, naturally becoming better and better all the time. Comedian Kumail Nanjiani has a rad bit about how games are the only medium that are better now than they've ever been. It's very funny, like all his work, but it's also illustrative of the way we talk and think about games.

So here's a thing: video games have a functionalism problem. That is, we treat change as natural. We assume that things are how they are for a Good Reason, that of course games look the way they do, because how else would they look? But! The field of science and technology studies tells us that technological conventions come to ascendancy for often completely accidental, unlikely historical reasons. There's a catchall term for this kind of dynamic: path dependence. It describes the way that small differences in initial conditions can lead to huge differences in uptake and success down the line.

So when we're thinking about sex in games, I don't think it's enough to look at the way things are right now. We've got to think historically about the conditions under which the technologies and conventions around video games formed, because these conditions continue to inform video games today.

Some of the earliest video games were based on pen-and-paper role-playing games like Dungeons & Dragons, which themselves were based on tabletop wargames. In Dungeons & Dragons and similar RPGs, the players take on the roles of adventurers in Western fantasy settings. You know the types: knights and rogues and wizards. The usual suspects.

These kinds of games can play totally differently depending

on the personalities and interests of the players. But, here is the thing: D&D is undeniably focused on personal combat with like, swords and magic missiles and junk. The game is built around fighting: fighting with orcs, fighting with other people who want your stuff, and sometimes even fighting with your friends. Some of the earliest experimenters with video games were really into D&D and similar RPGs, so much so that their games borrowed elements from the genre.

Moving through the '80s and '90s, RPGs became an incredibly popular genre. In a lot of these games, the story unfolds pretty linearly, punctuated by a series of combat challenges. It's kind of like if a fantasy novel was interrupted every once in a while by repetitive, frustrating tests that had nothing to do with the narrative.

Combat is typically the most mechanically developed interaction in the game. Players make decisions about equipment, battle strategy, and managing their party's health, items, and magic. Sometimes, the player can make decisions while they're talking to other characters, or they can do things like fishing or item-crafting, but combat is overwhelmingly the focus.

As genres like RPGs became popular, development practices and tools accrued around them. Some people got better at making them, and it became easier for other people to make them too. *Doom* was one of the earliest popular first-person games, and its model of shooting as the primary means of interacting with the world can still be felt in the tight association between first-person perspectives in games and shooting, to the point that first-person games that don't involve guns are still seen as curiosities by a lot of people. The point is that the current plausibility of (made-up) titles like *Manshooter X* and *Dungeon Lad's Quest* has a lot more to do with chance historical developments than we tend to assume.

It's easy to look at contemporary games and say that the reason so many of them are about violence and so few are about sex is because violence is easier to model—it's easier to ray-cast a bullet's path than to animate an embrace. But we need to remember that development technologies aren't neutral; they're informed by the interests of their creators, often in subtle and totally unpredictable ways.

In his satirical piece "Why So Few Violent Games?", Gregory Avery-Weir points out how contemporary game development engines might make it easier for developers to model violence than to model sex, but that's not because there's anything intrinsic about these two phenomena. It's because of the ways the values of early game developers have been encoded into the technologies they set in motion.

Where We Are Now

When we take cultural and technological contexts together, it seems to me that video games have formed a kind of feedback loop. The earliest games modeled violence, so systems evolved encouraging the development of games where violence was the central mechanic. Then as games came to occupy a more visible position in popular culture, especially around their depictions of violence, we came to see them as being about competition and conflict by nature. Which means that anyone looking to make a game about relationships or sex today faces a double challenge: a lack of technical support for their work, as well as the idea that games are mainly about some form of goal-directed competition.

Possible responses to this double challenge include producing a game about sex that takes on the dominant form of video games, then relegating sex to a background role, or rejecting received ideas and making a game about sex that is playful but not overtly goal directed.

Alternatives

I've already brought up some examples of games that attempt to include sex without altering the goal-oriented structures of contemporary video games, including examples that actually exploit the parallels between our cultural understandings of games and sex. But what about games where sexuality is incorporated in ways that disrupt these understandings? It's clear that bringing sex into games is a tough thing to do, but there are glimmers of change in both mainstream games and among smaller indie developers.

Mainstream: *Saints Row IV*

The *Saints Row* series started as a *Grand Theft Auto* derivative—an open-world game where the player is dropped in a city and given missions and tools to accomplish them with. This usually involves stealing cars and shooting everyone. But by the third game, the series took a parodic turn; by the fourth, you're fighting aliens inside a Matrix-like simulation of Earth where you have superpowers. Oh, and you're the president of the United States.

It's a pretty well-regarded series. But one of the reasons I like it so much—one that doesn't get discussed as often as some of its other features—is that it plays with sexuality in some interesting ways.

As a part of its attack on the conventions of contemporary mainstream games, *Saints Row IV* includes romance mechanics. These kinds of features are pretty strongly associated with Western role-playing games, and they usually play out like this: the player chooses a nonplayer character object of interest early on, the player chooses a series of obvious correct dialogue choices to ingratiate themselves with that character over the course of the game, the player sleeps with that character at the game's climax in an awkward softcore porn sequence, and finally the player receives an achievement for completing a relationship quest. Again, these games have been praised for their focus on human interactions and inclusion of queer characters, but they portray romantic and sexual relationships in instrumental ways. Sex is the goal, and you get there by telling someone everything they want to hear. Gross.

In *Saints Row IV*, you hang out with your friends on a big spaceship in between fighting aliens, much like in more serious fare like *Mass Effect*. You can walk around the ship and approach any of your compatriots at any time, and when you do, you're given two options. One key is labeled, "Speak with ____," and another is labeled, "Romance ____." This presentation is emblematic of the game's irreverence toward established conventions, reducing hours of dialogue selections to a single button press. And when you do press the romance button, what you get is a brief cutscene between the two characters in which they decide to fuck, the screen fades to black, and then it's over. But nothing's really changed on the ship—you can do this with anyone you want, if you like. In a way, the game encourages you to—the extremely brief conversations between your character and the others are well written and often very funny.

It's a simple move, but it effectively shifts sex to being an everyday, normal, maybe even kind of boring thing that isn't the ultimate goal of your character but is just a part of their daily life. Later in the game, you might get in a car and sing along to the radio with a character you fucked earlier, or fight hordes of aliens alongside them. None of your relationships are elevated to partner status regardless of how many times you sleep together, and no one is ever jealous—in this respect, maybe it's kind of unrealistic, but, if so, it's at least a kind of aspirational unrealism, a model of sexuality that seems so much healthier and more radical than that depicted in games like *Mass Effect* that emphasize romantic possession and position sex as the climax of a long courtship.

Sex here isn't a quest or a minigame; it's not part of the goal structure of the game at all. It's true that *Saints Row* doesn't depict sex mechanically—but it doesn't have to. And actually, by de-emphasizing sex as a goal and refusing to allow the player monogamous relationships, the game mirrors a queer politic of deprivileging romantic relationships and elevating friend relationships. In other words, this means trying to treat everyone we're close to in our lives with the same respect and tenderness that heteronormative culture tells us to reserve for our One True

Love. In this sense, *Saints Row IV* does more interesting work around sex than the games it's satirizing.

Independent Artists

Outside of the mainstream industry, independent artists and designers are doing all kinds of interesting things with sex and eroticism in games. It's impossible not to mention Twine here, the tool for making text-based games. It's incredibly accessible and has been used by all kinds of people to make all kinds of games since it was popularized in 2012 by anna anthropy's book *Rise of the Videogame Zinesters*. The neat thing about having accessible game creation tools is that nontraditional authors are using them to make nontraditional games. And it turns out that when you give people the means to make their own games? A lot of them are about sex—and kinds of sex that are unlikely to find their way into mainstream games anytime soon.

Take *Reset*, a game by Lydia Neon that basically asks what BDSM would be like in a world where most people had computers implanted in their brains. What's the most intimate, vulnerable, and exciting thing you could do in a world like that? Neon's answer is: you give control of your brain to your domme. The really interesting thing about *Reset* for me, and what makes it stand out as a work of hypertext, is the way the game immerses the player in the role of the character. Neon uses the second person "you," but also color changes, garbled text, and language modifications to simulate the experience of having your brain computer reset and recalibrated, and to emphasize the power exchange involved. Depending on the player, the sex might be hot, awkward, or alarming—but Neon incorporates a safeword into the game's narrative, so the player can end the scene at any point if it gets too intense for them.

Most of my games about sex and relationships have been made in Twine, too. One of the best things about the tool is the way it lets you bring a game from start to finish really quickly—so you can do things like make games as gifts, or respond to current events.

positive space was made as a gift. It's a game about intimacy between trans bodies that I made for my lover, a written narrative about the first night we spent together. Using Twine, I spliced together that story with excerpts from a zine by Miranda Bellwether called *Fucking Trans Women. FTW* coined the term "muffing" for the sex act of penetrating the inguinal canals—look it up if you're not sure what those are—and it was the first place that a lot of trans women had ever heard of the concept. The game included diagrams, text, and pictures from the zine. It was supposed to be hot, sincere, and educational. A love letter for my partner, sex edutainment for everyone else. A rad thing about it was that when it got picked up by game sites, some commenters mentioned that they'd actually learned something new about their bodies by playing it—something they probably wouldn't have learned anywhere else.

Consensual Torture Simulator was inspired by real-life romantic events too, but it was also a response to the treatment of violence in video games. When *Grand Theft Auto V* made headlines in fall 2013 for including a scene where the player tortures someone for information, I was like, cool, edgy. Except that it was 2013 and hyperviolence was, and still is, the unquestioned norm for video games. What would actually be edgy or new for games, I realized, was a game where you were hurting someone who wanted to be hurt.

In *CTS*, the player takes on the role of a dominant character in an established romantic relationship with a strong BDSM component. The player character and her lover set a goal in the introductory narrative of inflicting enough pain through impact play (involving hands, canes, etc.) to make the lover cry. But the player's free to end the scene at any time—even before delivering a single blow—and there's no penalty for doing that.

There is no bad ending if the player continues on past the onset of tears, or if they end the scene without meeting the established goal. It's very deliberately a game where it's impossible to fail in a meaningful sense, because I wasn't interested in exploring failure. *CTS* is about relationships, trust, and intimacy, and while it tracks the player's actions, it only does that to communicate ideas about these topics. A goal is present, but it doesn't represent ultimate victory and is always up for revision.

Part of my goal with the game was to comment on the state of video games, and to talk about the problems with fantasy hyperviolence. I wanted to show that hitting someone, inflicting violence, is work—that bodies aren't the inexhaustible machines that most games depict them as. The player has to be aware not only of her bottom's condition, but her own condition overall.

But also, I wanted to make a game about kink that wasn't overly serious, that was sweet and showed two characters who love each other. I have a vested interest in this. And while the game's reception in games circles was pretty good, I did get some pushback from people who couldn't wrap their head around the idea of consensual torture, who insisted that anyone who liked playing with power dynamics was messed up. Oddly, I wouldn't expect a lot of these people to have any problems with the kinds of nonconsensual violence that happen in games like *Grand Theft Auto*.

But listen: I'm a gay woman who likes my partners to slap and boss me around. That doesn't make me broken or damaged or brainwashed. It's okay if you don't understand it—I don't understand why people pay to see horror movies. But don't you think it's a little sad that violence goes more or less unquestioned in games until it's consensual? Don't you think it's depressing that we're overwhelmingly still more okay with violence than sex in games overall? I do, and I'm trying to change that.

Beyond these reasons for making *CTS*, I think BDSM is a particularly interesting way of approaching sex in games because kink is itself a form of play, with rules often explicitly set by participants in a way that, at its best, models a kind of consent conspicuously absent from dominant understandings of sexuality. A playful approach to the notion of winners and losers, with these roles sometimes predetermined, makes BDSM and kink structures useful to think about for anyone interested in producing games about sex.

Interactive fiction is just one way that artists are exploring sex in games. Artists like Paolo Pedercini have incorporated sex into games like *Queer Power,* a piece that uses the form of traditional fighting games to explore the fluidity of gender and desire. Fighting games are usually about knocking your opponent's health bar down to zero, but *Queer Power* is ambiguous about its goals, leaving its players free to explore different styles of play.

Also really exciting to me is the movement toward abstraction and uses of nonrepresentational images to convey sexuality, eroticism, and intimate relationships through play. Tale of Tales' *Luxuria Superbia* is a rad example of a game that eschews literal representation for suggestive metaphor. The player careens down a bright tunnel, stroking the walls in response to textual messages requesting and sometimes demanding the player's touch. Some people experience it as awkward, others as deeply erotic. The game was originally produced for touchscreens, so I read it as inviting us not just to play, but to think about our semi-erotic connections to these kinds of devices.

Stephen "increpare" Lavelle is another prolific designer whose work often deals with the sexual. *Slave of God* is one of my favorites by him. It's a first-person game that drops the player into a super loud, energetic nightclub. While first person games have become synonymous with the drive toward photorealism, *Slave of God* rejects this ideal in favor of bombarding the player with color and light, simulating sensory overwhelm and the ecstatic experience of making a connection with a stranger on a dance floor.

The game has a distinct ending triggered through a specific series of actions on the behalf of the player. But there are no fail states, and it's perfectly possible to simply experience the sensation of the game without completing any specific tasks. It's a game about sexuality and eroticism in a broad sense that takes advantage of the spatial dynamics of the first-person genre to place the player in a state that might be experienced as anxious, ecstatic, or something in between.

Because of the freedoms afforded artists who aren't making games for mass audiences, independent games are where most of the interesting work around sexuality is happening. The most exciting thing about it, for me, is that a lot of these games are being made by women and queers—people whose relationships to sex and play often looks a lot different from the mainstream model.

Future Directions

We're starting to explore sex in games, but so far it's been slow going. Thinking about the cultural associations we carry and the tech histories that have led up to today's game development context, this isn't actually all that surprising. But how can games continue to grow and to incorporate and comment on sex in new and useful ways?

Unlike some proponents of hardware improvements, I don't think better graphics or engines are the answer. Games have a photorealism problem—mainstream games in particular have become so focused on emulating film that the industry has come to believe the highest calling of video games is to visually reproduce reality perfectly. Generally speaking, but especially when it comes to making games about sex and eroticism, I don't think this is a very promising direction.

I'm excited about tools like Twine that are making it possible for new kinds of authors to make games about forms of sex and kinds of relationships that are totally underrepresented. And I'm stoked about the turn away from photorealism among independent artists who are choosing to explore eroticism in less literal ways.

What else? I see a huge potential for crossovers between video games and feminist and queer porn, whose producers already have a lot of experience thinking about new media and representation. And what about alternate reality games designed to encourage players to explore their relationships to sex, bodies, and communities? Can we imagine going beyond games about sex that are experienced by individual players at their keyboards to games that are dispersed and practiced by groups of players at once?

Of course, here we get into the fraught territory of gamification, and it's easy to imagine behavioralist nightmares of quantifying the sexual self in pursuit of the "improvement" of sexual experience. But what if games could be used to bolster broader queer struggles? We're only now beginning to explore the idea that a game could be erotic, but what about a game that encourages people to fuck and to push back against the shaming of non-normative sex?

These are possibilities that we are only starting to explore. Ultimately, confronting the question of sex in video games requires us to confront some of our most deeply held assumptions about the medium. If we want to make video games about sex that explore intimacy, play, and human connection rather than simply the mechanical processes involved, it'll have to be a part of a larger project of revising our ideas about what games are and can do.

merritt kopas is a multimedia artist and game designer. Her games include LIM *and* Consensual Torture Simulator.

The God in the Machine: Occultism, Demiurgic Theology, and Gnostic Self-Knowledge in Japanese Video Games*

OLA WIKANDER

Video games have always been entwined with science fiction and fantasy, but also with occult and religious themes. In this essay, Ola Wikander details Judeo-Christian influences on Japanese video games, relating them to a zeitgeist that put its mark on a handful of major works and that continues to define popular culture.

WE WERE A STRANGE BUNCH, PART OF A GENERATION THAT found our greatest cultural expression through roleplaying games, stories of alternative spirituality, tales of the occult, fantasy fiction, Japanophilia, and—last but certainly not least—video games. We were, in a way, a movement and we didn't even know it.

When you get into your thirties, you start noticing the strange interconnections that seem to exist between various interests

---

* I would like to extend a heartfelt thank you to my wife, Rebecca Bugge, with whom I have endlessly discussed most of the games mentioned in this article—and played them, of course!

in your life. As I was growing up, I looked at the world around me and found it lacking. Instead of embracing the seemingly unchanging roles that sports and "normal" youth culture presented, I—like many others—sought and found escapist bliss in the typically alternative cultural sources of the day, pen-and-paper roleplaying games and video games, for example. As I grew older, and while studying ancient languages, the history of religion, and Old Testament exegesis, I started to notice how many of the themes and motifs I had relished during my "popular culture upbringing" in fact provided examples of modern reception of old ideas derived from some of the very texts I was studying. I realized how many of my own interests—both as a scholar and as a consumer of cultural products—was a product of the *zeitgeist* in which I grew up.

I was born in 1981, which means that my years of cultural programming happened in the 1990s—a decade "both wonderful and strange," as Special Agent Dale Cooper would put it. The Generation X-ers that were a bit older resorted to irony and cool indifference as a method of defining themselves, which lead to a sort of laid-back lack of passion turned into an aesthetic credo. But there was another type of cultural attitude that came into vogue in that decade, namely what I like to refer to as the "Dark '90s" (or, to be honest, "Dark '90s-Plus," since the attitudes to which I am referring survived into the early 2000s).* I use this expression to describe those products of popular culture of the age that were not in any sense ironic, but rather dystopian, bleak, and paranoid.

---

* I make no claims for the originality of this phrase. For example, one comes across it and similar expressions to describe developments in comic books during the '90s.

The '90s abounded in tales of government conspiracies, dark secrets, and the sinister machinations of "those in power." In line with the questioning and disillusioned spirit of the era, those dark forces could rarely be identified with the classic boogey-men of earlier times (imperialists, capitalists, communists, etc.); the imagined enemy tended to be much more nebulous, or up in the air. Sometimes this could be taken as a metaphor, some-times it was literal. In the first case, I mean stories in which the enemy consisted of shadow governments and similar shady institutions—one of the most well-known examples of this was, of course, the TV series *The X-Files*, which ran significantly enough between 1993 and 2002. The series, with its classical yet extremely convoluted storyline about alien invasion, shadowy machinations, and medical experimentation, sums up the Dark '90s ethos extremely well.

There were also stories in which the enemy was a supernat-ural power, often bearing similarities to the Judeo-Christian God. The '90s was the decade during which the rediscovery of Gnosticism truly seeped into popular culture and started to influence movies, books, pen-and-paper roleplaying games, and—as we shall see—Japanese video games.

The typical Dark '90s story features conspiracy theories and unseen organizations trying to manipulate world politics—or even the metaphysical mechanics of the world itself—for their purposes. One common trope was that of the manufactured super-soldier; this appeared suitably enough in *The X-Files*, in which parts of the story involved both sinister medical exper-iments, super-soldiers, and alien invasion. In the video game world, the *Metal Gear Solid* series is an excellent and ongoing example of this type of tale of shadow governments and genetically engineered super-soldiers.[*] But sometimes the conspirators were more spiritual in nature.

During the '90s, it seemed as though a religious fervor was sweeping through the world of Japanese gaming—a dark and twisted fervor that reinterpreted many cultural icons of the Western religious world. Suddenly concepts and imagery related to Judeo-Christian symbolism abounded. Of course, Japanese video gaming was and is replete with references to Asian religious traditions, such as Buddhism and Shintō,[†] but here I will concentrate on the much more surprising appearance of themes and motifs from Western occult and religious traditions. The reception and adaptation of Western religious imagery constitutes an interesting example of cultural interaction, especially when it occurs in a culture like the Japanese, which is often stereotypically regarded as being very secularized, whether that is actually true in practice or not. The influence of Western religions on Japanese gaming illustrates how complex the role of religion in Japan really can be.

One common example of this consisted in symbols associated with Kabbalah, the classical tradition of Jewish mysticism, which often appeared in Japanese video games in the '90s and the beginning of the 2000s. The imported material was, however, sometimes superficial in the sense that the actual ideological or

---

[*] The Metal Gear Solid series also includes complex reflections on the relationship between the player and the played—of a sort reminiscent of the games discussed at the end of this article. As is often pointed out, Metal Gear Solid 2: Sons of Liberty (released in 2001) constitutes a truly postmodern take on these questions.

[†] And, in certain cases, Hinduism, for example in Rudora no Hihō (often translated Treasure of the Rudras), released in 1996.

theological bases of the imagery had little impact on the games. One of the most famous examples of this rather shallow borrowing of Kabbalistic imagery can be found in one of the most successful Japanese games ever, *Final Fantasy VII* (released for the Sony PlayStation in 1997). This game constitutes a virtual extravaganza of '90s mainstays: a corrupt company, genetic engineering, etc. The story is not theological in the Judeo-Christian sense of the word (such themes are, however, prominent in the CGI movie sequel to the game, *Advent Children*).

Despite the lack of Western theology in the game itself, the creators (presumably the main architects of the game, Kazushige Nojima and/or Tetsuya Nomura) could not resist adding a blatant reference to the Kabbalah-laden popular culture of the '90s—in the form of one of the most iconic of all video game villains: Sephiroth. His name is identical with that of the ten emanations of God in Kabbalistic philosophy. The ten Sephirot(h) occur as early in the history of Kabbalah as the *Sepher Yĕṣîrâ* ("Book of Creation," probably from the early Middle Ages). It is, however, possible that the use of the term for the antagonist in *Final Fantasy VII* did not have its direct origin in Jewish sources. This is perhaps suggested by the spelling of the name Sephiroth: the Classical Hebrew language did indeed feature a *th* sound at the end of this word, but in Modern Hebrew the sound has changed and the word has become *Sefirot* or *Sephirot*, with a simple *t*. The older spelling with *th* is common in sources relating to Western occultism or esotericism, especially those related to the tradition started by The Hermetic Order of the Golden Dawn, a British magical order founded in the late 1800s. Occult and Golden Dawn-related material was quite common in certain parts of popular culture during the '90s and could be part of the path the word took before ending up in a Japanese video game.

Japanese video games from the '90s and early 2000s (and, for that matter, other Japanese popular culture genres, such as anime) often include references to Western esotericism, occultism, or alternative religion. The same phenomenon is found in other art forms as well—for example, the sister series to *The X-Files, Millennium,* included many references to such ideas. This reception of esoteric and occult material in popular culture—during an age that is often regarded as being very secularized—has been noted in modern scholarship as being expressions of a greater "occulture."* Such references have continued to appear; one example is the 2011 game *El Shaddai: Ascension of the Metatron,* which borrows its background story from the apocryphal *First Book of Enoch,* a text that has long been popular in esoteric circles for its descriptions of the beings often known as *Nephilim,* hybrids born of spiritual beings and human women.†

As mentioned earlier, *Final Fantasy VII* was a perfect example of a Dark '90s story in other respects as well: the villain Sephiroth was a sort of cloned super-soldier made from genetic material gathered from a crashed alien being known as *Jenova.* As has been pointed out many times, the name Jenova is probably meant to evoke the divine name Jehova (possibly combined

---

* This term was popularized by Christopher Partridge in his book *The Re-Enchantment of the West: Alternative Spiritualities, Sacralization, Popular Culture and "Occulture"* (2004).

† The term *Nephilim* appears for the first time in Genesis 6:4; from there it was borrowed into the Book of Enoch.

with Latin *nova*, either in its literal sense of "new", as in "new God," or simply to create resonance with the word "supernova"—the being does, after all, fall from the sky).*

Other than this, the theological elements of the game appear more New Age in style: the central concept is the "Lifestream," an almost hypostasized version of "all the life in the universe," which actually acts almost as a character in the story.

Whereas *Final Fantasy VII* does not itself include much Western theology (despite the overt religious reference of the name Sephiroth), such thinking was certainly not far from the minds of the creators. The follow-up animated movie, *Advent Children*, really goes over the top in tying itself to Christian imagery. The heroine Aerith, who tragically dies in the game, here appears as a figure very easy to interpret as a reference to the Roman Catholic Madonna.† The movie actually ends with what appears to be a mass baptism, when the main protagonist Cloud Strife purifies the titular children from an alien miasmic infection that has infested the Lifestream. The story in the movie is to a large extent one of redemption—the protagonist has to overcome the grief and guilt he feels over the death of Aerith—and this redemptive development is finally brought about through

---

* For example, this is the explanation one finds in the "Jenova" article of the online *Final Fantasy* Wiki (not Wikipedia, but a separate project). The Wiki is quite a comprehensive source that also notes, for example, Gnostic influences on *Final Fantasy X* and other religious themes in the series (some of which are mentioned in this article). The connection between "Jehova" and "Jenova" is also argued in Robert Wedin's 2014 master's thesis, *Video Games and Contemporary Esotericism: A Study of Eco-Spirituality and the Grand Polemical Narrative in Final Fantasy VII* (Gothenburg University).

† Although one could also imagine a reference to the (usually) female Buddhist *bodhisattva*, Kannon, being present as well.

the agency of the Madonna-like figure herself. This example of the reception of Christian imagery in Japanese gaming is challenging from a methodological point of view, since it occurs not in the game but as part of a movie sequel; yet it was, however, created by many of the same people that were involved in the game itself and is also computer animated, thus providing visual continuity. The game *Final Fantasy VII* was published for the Sony PlayStation in 1997, at a point when polygonal 3D real-time graphics were rather primitive; the characters look "blocky," and the story leaves a lot to the visual imagination. The *Advent Children* movie came out in 2005 and used modern and prerendered 3D modelling—thus it could well be argued that the movie shows us what the characters and settings of the game were really meant to look like. From a narrative standpoint, this poses an interesting question: Are the theological themes present in the movie to be retroactively read into the game itself?

There is one Judeo-Christian literary trope that spread widely in Japanese gaming during the '90s and early 2000s that actually did, and still does, carry a great deal of theological weight. This is the idea of the "rebellion against the gods," or against God in the singular. As mentioned earlier, this theme no doubt owed much to one very surprising religio-historical trend: the rediscovery of ancient Gnosticism.

In popular culture, this rediscovery took place in the '80s and '90s due in large part to the popularization of the writings from the Nag Hammadi library, a treasure trove of Coptic manuscripts from late Antiquity, discovered in 1945 at Nag Hammadi, in Egypt. The discovery of these texts gave modern scholarship direct large-scale access to the writings of ancient Gnostic religions* for the first time, and during the '90s, one starts to see a large number of references to ideas from these ancient texts surface in popular culture. Elaine Pagels' popular book, *The Gnostic Gospels*, originally published in 1979, was an important factor in the popularization of ancient Gnostic thought in the modern world, bringing it to a wider audience. When we reach the '90s and early 2000s, Gnostic themes and motifs occur frequently in popular culture, as has been noted many times,[†] and not least in video games, a medium which is especially well-suited to expressing the type of philosophical questions provoked by Gnostic thought.

Although Gnosticism as a meta-category has been shown to be a difficult and unclear concept, one can note certain common traits among the ancient forms of religion lumped together under this umbrella. They are mostly based on a Jewish or Christian background—often using biblical stories and imagery as a

---

*   Using the term "Gnostic" as a term for a set of ancient Christian (and, to some extent, non-Christian) movements is a practice not without its problems. In recent years, there has been a gradual reappraisal of the term, with scholars accepting there was never one Gnosticism, but rather a set of divergent movements that shared certain characteristics with each other, such as a negative view of the material world and a wish to be liberated from it, and a rather negative view of the "lower deity" (or "Demiurge") responsible for creating that world. One should note that the description of Gnostic theology given above is cursory indeed and not necessarily typical of all movements of ancient Gnosticism. Because of the problems of defining Gnosticism, there have even been attempts to do away with the term entirely; the most well-known attempt in this direction is the book *Rethinking 'Gnosticism': An Argument for Dismantling Dubious Category* by Michael Allen Williams (1996).

†   Two of the most overt examples of appropriation of Gnostic motifs in modern popular culture are the *Matrix* movies and the pen-and-paper roleplaying game *Kult*. Typically enough, *Kult* was originally released in 1991, and the first *Matrix* movie in 1999, encompassing the whole of the Dark '90s.

backdrop for religious and philosophical speculation. However, the Gnostic religions typically express a very different perspective on the Old Testament stories of creation than the standard Judeo-Christian readings.

Central to the various Gnostic movements is the idea that the present, material world is fundamentally not a very good place to be, and that the human species does not really belong here. Humanity is, according to many Gnostic sources, in reality purely spiritual, and our presence in the material world is a cause for grief. We wander around in this world, not remembering who we really are, constantly subject to pain, sickness, confusion—and ultimately death. The reason for this sad state of affairs is not sin, in the way often imagined in Christian theology, but a lack of spiritual insight or knowledge. The world is in truth emanated from the supreme deity himself, but we have forgotten its origin and lesser spiritual powers have created this material world as a sort of prison for humanity. Human beings are alien to this world, fallen into matter from a higher state of existence. Often, the Gnostic religions have a rather negative view of the creator of the physical universe, the so-called Demiurge, who is not to be identified with the supreme deity, but is seen either as a slightly incompetent middleman, or as a malevolent false god who actively tries to keep humanity from discovering its origin.

In the classical analysis of Gnostic religions, the concept that is thought to save humanity from this fallen world is not belief but knowledge, known in Greek as *Gnōsis*. This is the knowledge of "who we were, what we have become, where we were, or where we have been thrown, where we hasten, whence we are freed, what birth is, and what rebirth is."* When the human being rediscovers who he or she really is—a part of the divine, spiritual, and nonmaterial world—then liberation is won. In many systems of Gnosticism, this knowledge is granted through the appearance of a savior figure from without, an alien, so to speak, who enters the world of matter to awaken sleeping humanity.† In Christian Gnosticism, this savior figure is usually identified as Jesus Christ. A beautiful iteration of this type of Gnostic savior myth can be found in the so-called "Naassene Psalm," which is not preserved as part of the Nag Hammadi Library, but was known prior to the discovery of those texts. The "Naassene Psalm" says of the human soul:

> Sometimes she gains mastery and glimpses light,
> or she plunges into evil misery and weeps.
> Sometimes she is mourned and is happy,
> or she weeps and is condemned.
> Then she is judged and finally dies.
> Sometimes she is misled down a labyrinth of evils,
> trapped in a corner with no way out.
>
> Jesus said, Look, father, she is wandering the earth
> and evil is trying to catch her.
> She is wandering far from your breath.

---

*   This classical definition of *Gnōsis* comes from the fragments preserved from the writings of Theodotus, the second century Valentinian Gnostic theologian (*Fragmenta ex Theodoto* 78:2).

†   It is certainly no coincidence that there are at least two ancient Gnostic texts called *Allogenēs*, the Greek word for "Foreigner" or "Alien."

She is trying to flee the bitter chaos and knows no
   escape.
O father, send me to her.
I will descend, carrying the seals.
I will wander through all the aeons and uncover
   all the mysteries.
I will disclose the forms of the gods.
And I will teach the secrets of the holy way
whose name is Gnosis.*

There is an interesting relationship that can be imagined between this type of Gnostic mythology and the role of the video game player in relation to the character he or she plays. Just like the fallen human soul described by Gnostic religions, the video game player steps into a false world that only exists for as long as one believes in it. The player is the "stranger" or "alien" who rules his or her avatar in an illusionary world, and, at least in most cases, tries to help the constructed character. But beside these general philosophical similarities, there are a number of cases in which Japanese video games of the '90s and early 2000s took up Gnostic themes and motifs, then used them to speculate about the relationship between the player, the played, and the video game itself. The idea of a rebellion against false gods that stands at the core of much Gnostic mythology has become a mainstay of video game narratives.

---

* I have quoted the translation found in Willis Barnstone and Marvin Meyer (eds.), *The Gnostic Bible* (2003), pp. 493-494. The translation is based on earlier ones by Robert M. Grant and J.F. Henry, and was revised in its present form by Willlis Barnstone. The original Greek text is preserved as part of the work *Refutatio Omnium Haeresium* by the Church Father Hippolytus (5.6.3–11.1). I have quoted the main part of the psalm but have omitted the first few lines.

In Japanese gaming, the Gnostic and maltheistic trend prevalent in so much popular culture was wed with a perhaps secularist exotization of religion in general. The result was a trend, still ongoing, of stories concerned with repressive and shadowy divine or semi-divine powers, against which the protagonists must fight for the freedom of humanity (or its equivalent in the game universe).

Here again, the *Final Fantasy* series provides ample evidence. The tenth installment of the series (released for the PlayStation 2 in 2001) is based around this very idea. The plot of the game is quite convoluted, but at its center we find the idea of a false and antagonistic godlike being known as Yu Yevon, whose only objective is forever to keep alive the memory of his beloved city Zanarkand, which was destroyed a thousand years before the beginning of the game. As a result of this ambition, a dream version of Zanarkand is created and forcibly kept separate from the rest of the game world to prevent the other inhabitants from discovering the dream city and causing it harm. For the purpose of keeping the rest of the world at bay, Yu Yevon creates a vast, whale-like being called Sin, who continually destroys much of the game world in order to keep humanity at a low level of technological development.

The inhabitants of the game world have a way of stopping Sin temporarily, but the one who performs this task, known as a Summoner, has to sacrifice his or her life and turn one of his or her companions into a new Sin, thus perpetuating a vicious cycle. Around this concept, the population of the game world have built an entire religion of Yevonism, which appears to be a sort of conglomerate of Roman Catholicism and Japanese

Shintō; the only real purpose of this authoritarian religious hierarchy is to perpetuate the pilgrimages of the Summoners and to dissuade the populace from using high technology, which would add to their many sins, for which they must constantly try to make atonement. Criticism against religious antagonism towards technology is very apparent.

One may also note that Sin is an aquatic being who destroys the habitations of humanity by creating tsunami-like tidal waves. Through this narrative construct, the creators of the game have wed their theological tale with the very real fear of tsunamis and natural catastrophes in East Asia (the world of the game appears in many ways to be modeled to look vaguely South Pacific). This also creates an intertextual relationship with a prominent motif in the Judeo-Christian canon, specifically the Hebrew Bible—namely that of a terrible sea monster or dragon, Leviathan or Rahab, who threatens the world.[*] The triad of Sin, a Western-like church structure, and an aquatic chaos monster can be read as stemming from Judeo-Christian symbolism.

The central story of the game focuses on the struggle of the main characters to unmask Yevonism and finally to confront Yu Yevon himself. The motif of revolt against a false god moves to the forefront.

Further complicating the narrative picture of *Final Fantasy X* is the protagonist, a young sportsman character named Tidus. Tidus hails from the dream version of Zanarkand, and much of his personal development consists of his realization of his identity as being a part of a dream. Here again, we find a narrative

---

[*] For examples of this motif in the Hebrew Bible, see Ps 74:13-14, Ps 89:10-11, Job 3:8, and Job 26:12.

motif amenable to a Gnostic interpretation: Tidus has to wake up and understand that he is, himself, a part of the creation of the Demiurge-like false god Yu Yevon, and in so doing, he can aid in bringing about the salvation of the whole game world. In one crucial instance, however, the story of Tidus differs from the Gnostic myth mentioned above: Tidus actually *is* a created part of the false world, not just its prisoner. This means that becoming aware and doing the right thing becomes much more of a sacrifice. His struggle against his creator can only lead to his own erasure from existence, which, indeed, is what happens at the end of the game.[*]

The *Final Fantasy* series contains more examples of revolts against false gods. Both the twelfth and thirteenth installation of the series include similar motifs. In the case of *Final Fantasy XII*, the concept is further complicated by the fact that one of the godlike beings actually sides with humanity and wants to aid it in taking control of its own destiny. The Namco Bandai-produced game *Tales of Xillia* (2011) also features the motif.

The most overt reception of Gnostic terms and motifs in Japanese gaming is probably represented by the *Xenosaga* series, as well its "spiritual predecessor" *Xenogears*. The *Xenosaga* series includes numerous names taken from ancient Gnosticism, including a type of antagonist called The Gnosis. Mary Magdalene plays a central part in the narrative: she is reborn as an android! Here again, we find references to esoteric religious imagery without necessarily having a theology

---

[*] The direct sequel, *Final Fantasy X2* (not to be confused with *Final Fantasy XII*, which is a completely different game), provides an opportunity to recreate him, which is also hinted at in the very last scene of *X* itself—all's well that ends well!

attached to it, as with Sephiroth. Mary Magdalene does have a central role in certain Gnostic texts, and the modern popular cultural reception of Gnosticism has elevated this role, as evidenced in works such as *The DaVinci Code*, which has very little to do with Gnostic theology as such, but a lot to do with the conspiracy theory craze of the '90s and early 2000s.

The idea of a sometimes contentious relationship between a divine power and the main characters can be explored in a video game in ways rather different than other media. The reason for this is the nature of the gaming medium itself; a dichotomy between creator and created is built into its very fabric. To be sure, this duality can be very successfully exploited and played within literature and movies too, but the video game experience really pushes the question to its limits. The player of the game is by necessity a sort of ghost in the machine. He or she controls the main character(s) but is normally unseen. From the perspective of the characters, the player is either a god or an alien spirit, residing in another world but looking into the world of the simulation. The player is the gnostic stranger who really belongs somewhere else but has descended into a lower world. And, just as is the case in a number of religious philosophies (I am thinking especially of Vedāntist Hinduism), the false identification between the stranger and the created world exists only as long as one believes in it.

I have found it illuminating to perform the simplistic experiment of shutting the TV down while playing a game and just continuing to play blind, so to speak. This highlights that what one does while playing is nothing more than push arbitrary buttons on the controller. All the magic happens in the mind.

A video game *is* nothing in itself, just as written symbols on a page *are* nothing—until the "divine creator" makes it into reality—until we read into or make something out of them. Without the player, the game does not exist. Its characters are blind and soulless, in a way more acute than in any book or movie. Since every playthrough of a game is different (in some cases only marginally so, if the game is highly linear, but sometimes greatly so), the story does not exist until it is played out. To be sure, the main story of the game exists in the mind of the game creators, but the exact motions and actions of the characters are decided by the player.

The reader of a book is in one sense more passive—he or she creates private images of the story of the book, but these are to a large extent ruled by the author. By contrast, a gamer can often change the entire outcome of the story. If the creators of the game are its Demiurges, the player can be both God and alien savior.

All this puts the example of Tidus in *Final Fantasy X* in a strange light. The character in the game controlled by the player is, after all, revealed to be a dream created by an antagonistic god-like being—and subsequently disappears. What does this imply for the relationship between player and character? The character the player controls is revealed to be an unreal construct, even within the context of the game itself. He is not only unreal in relationship to us, the players, but to his friends in the game. His existence is dependent on someone else believing in it. This becomes, in a strange but illuminating way, a sort of conscious or unconscious comment on the relationship between the game and the person playing it.

When talking about the relationship between the creator and the created in Japanese video games, there is one work of art that should not be forgotten—and I use the term "art" deliberately. I am referring to *Deadly Premonition*, known in Japan as *Red Seeds Profile*, which was directed by eccentric video game *auteur* Hidetaka Suehiro, also known as SWERY, and released in 2010.

When released, this game was divisive among both reviewers and the public. On one hand, it was hailed as an absolute masterpiece, rightly in my view, while on the other hand, it was decried as a technical disaster. It ostensibly appears to be little more than a weird survival horror game heavily influenced by David Lynch and Mark Frost's TV-series *Twin Peaks*—many of its features remind one clearly of the series: a beautiful teenage girl is murdered in a small town in the Northwest US, an FBI agent is sent to investigate it, an occult story emerges, and many other reminiscent characters appear. The further one gets into the game, however, the more one realizes that it's no mere cult replica, but a piece of truly postmodern and philosophical speculative fiction, the immediate concern of which is something only gaming can embody so poignantly: the relationship between the governing mind and the governed body as projected through the dichotomy between the player and main character.

Among the many weird and wonderful features of *Deadly Premonition* is the fact that the main character, FBI agent Francis York Morgan, appears to have an invisible buddy, an unseen person called Zach, with whom he has recurrent dialogues during the course of the murder investigation that makes up the game. At the beginning of the story, Zach is not explained in any way; both the player and the other characters are understandably baffled at York's ubiquitous asides to his unseen companion. As the game progresses, it appears more and more as though Zach is a sort of metaphor for the player. York speaks to Zach in a way that implies that Zach controls him, in a way, or at least influences his actions to a large degree. This, in itself, is an innovative postmodern take on the conditions of gaming.

The plot thickens. When the game reaches its inevitable conclusion, it turns out the Zach persona—with whom the player has likely been unconsciously identifying—was the real one all along, not York. The York persona that had been displayed as the main character's identity was nothing but a construct or simulacrum of Zach's supernaturally infused subconscious. When Morgan confronts the main villain of the game—a demon masquerading as a seed salesman!—he is suddenly thrown into an epiphany of self-knowledge. The two personalities switch places, and the main character is suddenly Francis Zach Morgan. And even stranger—the townspeople suddenly treat him as though this had been the case all along. The identity we took for granted was a false one, perhaps a projection of the main character's fear.

When this switch occurs, it is much more than a multiple personalities trope *Fight Club*-style—"It was me all along!"—No, when Zach understands who he really is—that he is Zach and that York is the fake with whom he has been conversing all this time—the game implicitly switches the places of the player and the played, the ruler and the ruled, the creator and the created. The personality that we believed to be "us" was really "him" all along; the alien of the story is, in fact, its protagonist. In story terms, this is really the moment of redemption for Morgan. It is the point where knowledge destroys ignorance, where the dichotomy between creator and created is finally inverted. He is himself the "god of the game" that we, in all our vanity, believed ourselves to be. The personality with which we identified ourselves is the one locked in the game.

This type of deconstruction of the limit between the teller of the story and the one about whom the story is being told is only possible in the video game medium. Hidetaka Suehiro solidifies the very thing that makes gaming a completely unique artistic endeavor.

The bizarre inversion of the relationship between the player and the played in *Deadly Premonition* is made even more prominent by the fact that earlier in the game there are a number of scenes in which York speaks to Zach in private—they discuss, among other things, which one of them the female lead of the story, the police-woman Emily Wyatt, might be attracted to. In these conversations, the perspective becomes even more distorted: York (ostensibly the character in the game) says that Emily seems to be attracted to Zach (ostensibly the incorporeal character identified with the player). When playing the game, this appears ludicrous: How could the in-game character Emily possibly have any sort of relationship with York's invisible friend? When it is finally revealed that York was really the invisible friend all along, these scenes become, in a way, understandable, but with a weird twist. The lines spoken by York in those scenes have to be construed as not being spoken at all, only thought. These private scenes show the true relationship between the characters, whereas most of the game inverts their relationship.

All in all, *Deadly Premonition* challenges all preconceptions one might have about the relationship between the player and the played in video games. Who creates whom? In literature, it is quite possible, and sometimes fashionable, to play with the roles of reader, writer, and main character, but video games takes this dynamic further because of the implied identification between the one experiencing the work and the lead character in it.

The dialectic between the ruler and the ruled, the god in the machine and the being in the machine (so well deconstructed in *Deadly Premonition* and, to an extent, in *Final Fantasy X*) could almost be viewed as a strange present-day analogue of the master and slave dialectic of Hegelian philosophy.* The ruled one (the character in the game) gives over his sense of self to the player, but in some games, the dichotomy is inverted, and the played character starts questioning his or her own role in the drama.† As we have seen, this can be done using narrative implements drawn in part from Western theological history.

The loosely defined movement I was part of—the counter-cultural gaming community of the Dark '90s and its present-day descendants—was into much more than another possible take on late twentieth-century postmodern irony. Some of our ideas—and the popular culture on which we thrived—gradually turned out to be related to a vast background of philosophical

---

* The classical statement of this idea is found in Hegel's *Phenomenology of Spirit* (*Die Phänomenologie des Geistes*, published in 1807).

† As mentioned in an earlier footnote, a similar deconstruction of the relationship between the player and the played occurs in *Metal Gear Solid 2*, in which the main character seems at the end to rebel against the shadowy forces controlling him, implicitly questioning his own role as a character in a game. There, however, the occult or religious superstructure is lacking.

and religious thinking, going back to ancient Gnosticism and similar movements. As tends to be the case, no cultural phenomenon can be viewed in isolation. What appears to be entirely new can represent the transformation of earlier currents.

Video games are certainly not the only form of Dark '90s cultural production that show evidence of this reception of Gnostic and occult themes and motifs. One finds the same thing elsewhere, and not least in tabletop roleplaying games. The *zeitgeist* influenced many of the products we consumed. But video games are suited to expressing that *zeitgeist* in a manner difficult to match. They made us think about who the god in the machine really is, and they still do.